MW01630369

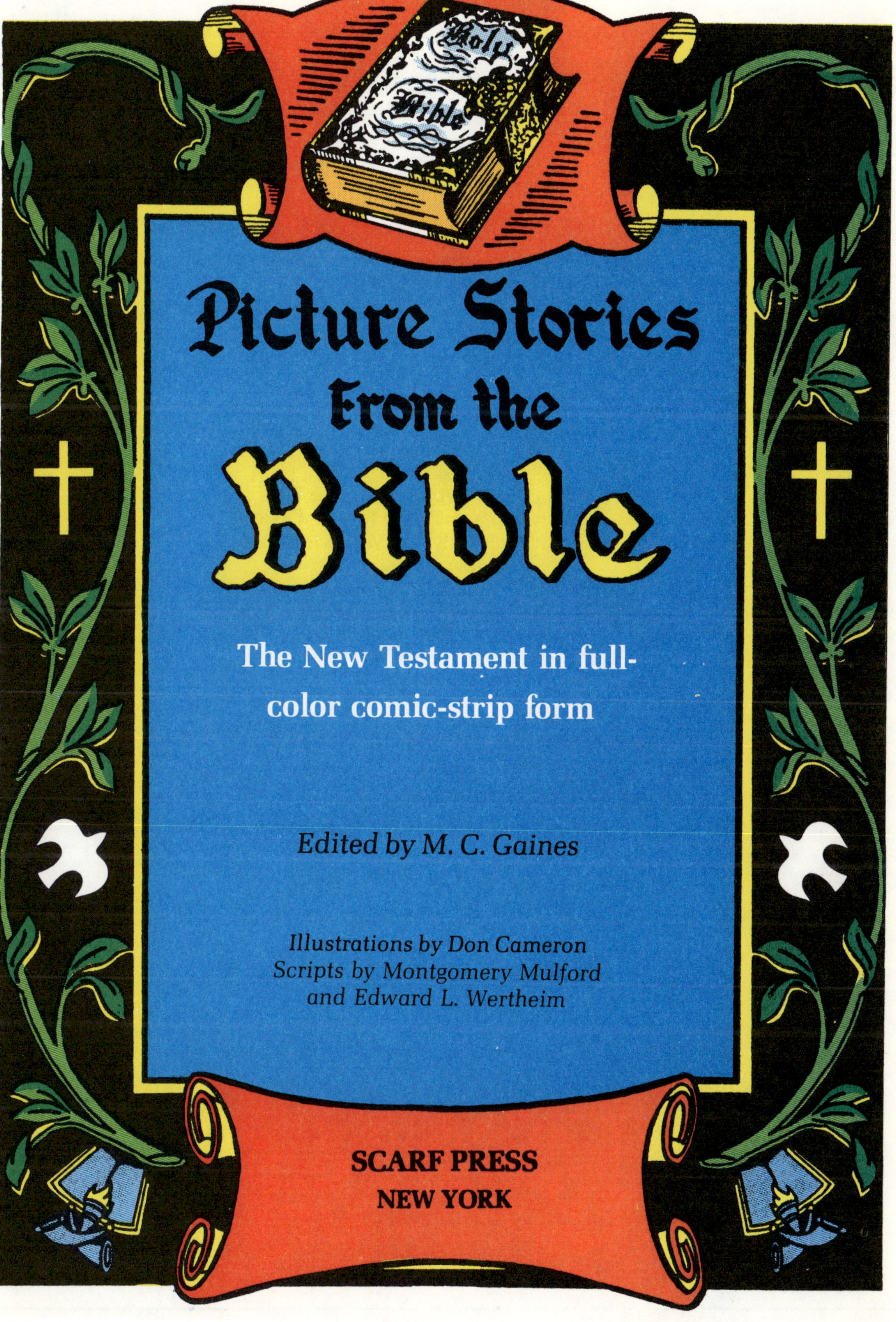
Holy Bible
Picture Stories
from the
Bible
The New Testament in full-color comic-strip form
Edited by M. C. Gaines
Illustrations by Don Cameron
Scripts by Montgomery Mulford
and Edward L. Wertheim
SCARF PRESS
NEW YORK

Published in the United States
and Canada by

Scarf Press
58 East 83rd Street
New York, New York 10028

Library of Congress Catalog Card Number: 80-51593
ISBN 0-934386-02-1

Printed in the United States of America
Color separations by Post Graphics Inc.

80 81 82 83 84   10 9 8 7 6 5 4 3 2 1

Featuring the Events in the Last Year of His Life

The Principal Events

Scripture References

MATTHEW

Chapter	Verses	Page
6	5-15	63
11	25-30	60
13	55	55
18	1-3	53
18	4-6	54
18	21-28	54
18	29-35	55
19	13-30	70
20	17-29	71
21	1-27	73
21	33-41	74
22	15-46	75
23	1-12	75
23	13-37	76
24	1-36	77
25	1-13	78
25	14-46	79
26	1-5	80
26	6-13	72
26	36-47	84
26	48-68	85
26	69-75	86
27	1-2	87
27	3-10	89
27	15-31	88
27	32	89
27	33-49	90
27	50-56	91
27	57-66	92
28	1-10	93
28	11-15	94
28	16	95
28	17-20	97

MARK

Chapter	Verses	Page
9	33-36	53
10	1	58
10	13-31	70
10	32-45	71
11	1-33	73
12	38-40	75
12	41-44	76
13	1-37	77
14	1-3	80
14	3-9	72
14	32-43	84
14	44-65	85
14	66-72	86
15	1-5	86
15	6-15	88
15	21	89
15	22-36	90
15	37-41	91
15	42-46	92
15	47	93
16	1-11	93
16	12-13	94
16	14	95
16	15-20	97

LUKE

Chapter	Verses	Page
9	46-48	53
9	51-62	58
10	1-24	60
10	25-34	61
10	35-42	62
11	1-13	63
11	37-54	64
14	1-14	66
15	1-32	67
17	11-19	69
18	9-14	69
18	15-30	70
18	31-34	71
19	1-10	71
19	29-40	73
21	1-4	76
21	5-36	77
22	1-6	80
22	39-47	84
22	48-53	85
22	54-71	86
23	1-16	87
23	17-25	88
23	26-30	89
23	32-45	90
23	46-49	91
23	50-54	92
23	55-56	93
24	1-12	93
24	13-35	94
24	36-43	95
24	44-53	97

JOHN

Chapter	Verses	Page
7	1-52	55
8	1-33	56
8	34-59	57
9	1-38	59
10	22-42	65
11	1-45	68
12	1-11	72
12	12-19	73
13	1-17	80
13	18-38	81
14	1-27	81
15	1-27	82
16	32-33	82
17	1-26	83
18	1-3	84
18	4-14	85
18	15-34	86
18	35-38	87
18	39-40	88
19	1-16	88
19	17	89
19	17-29	90
19	30-37	91
19	38-42	92
20	1-18	93
20	19-29	95
20	30-31	97
21	1-17	96

Part Three   THE STORY OF PETER, PAUL AND OTHER DISCIPLES
The Formation of the Early Christian Church

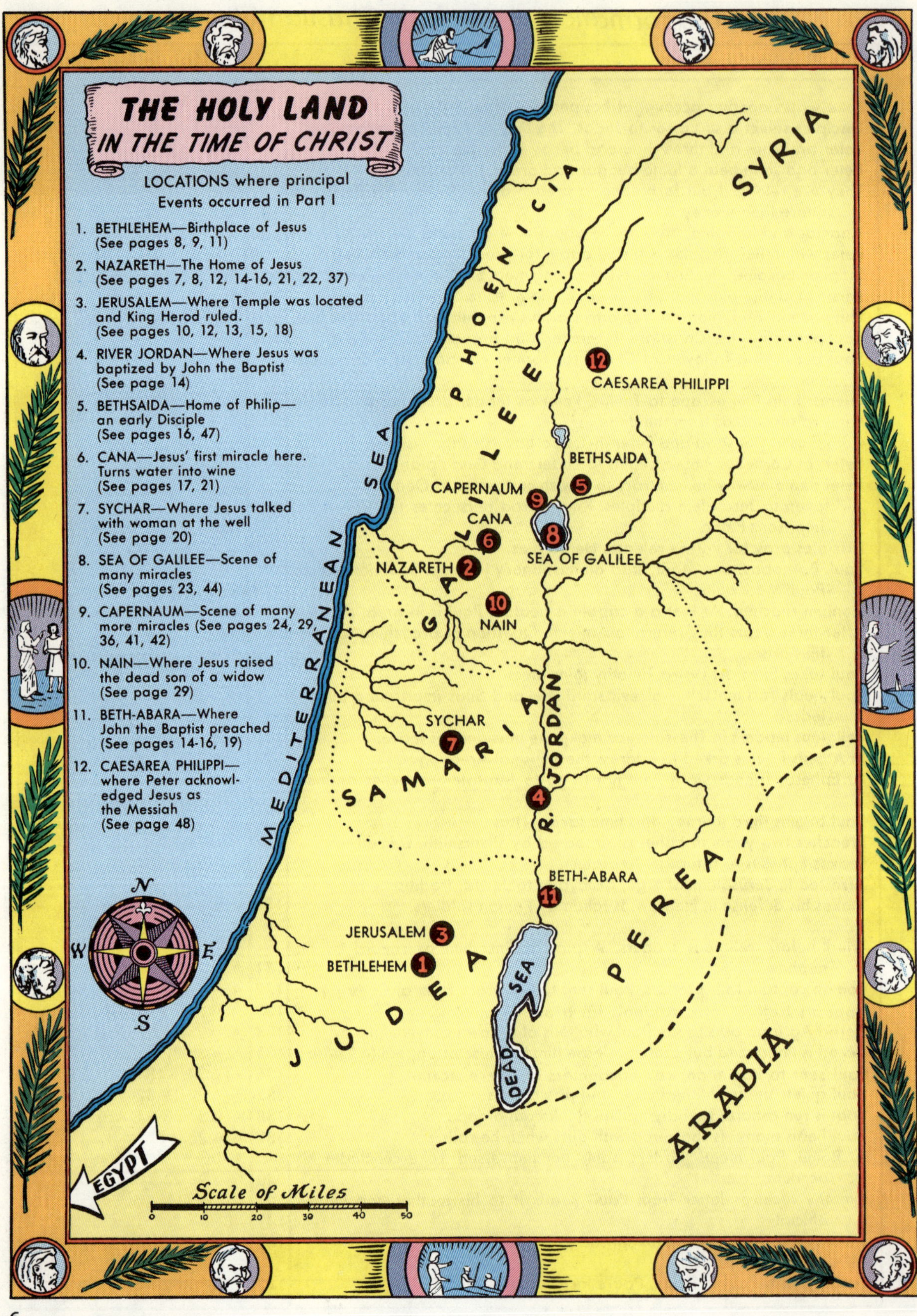

THE HOLY LAND
IN THE TIME OF CHRIST

LOCATIONS where principal
Events occurred in Part I

1. BETHLEHEM—Birthplace of Jesus
(See pages 8, 9, 11)

2. NAZARETH—The Home of Jesus
(See pages 7, 8, 12, 14-16, 21, 22, 37)

3. JERUSALEM—Where Temple was located
and King Herod ruled.
(See pages 10, 12, 13, 15, 18)

4. RIVER JORDAN—Where Jesus was
baptized by John the Baptist
(See page 14)

5. BETHSAIDA—Home of Philip—
an early Disciple
(See pages 16, 47)

6. CANA—Jesus' first miracle here.
Turns water into wine
(See pages 17, 21)

7. SYCHAR—Where Jesus talked
with woman at the well
(See page 20)

8. SEA OF GALILEE—Scene of
many miracles
(See pages 23, 44)

9. CAPERNAUM—Scene of many
more miracles (See pages 24, 29,
36, 41, 42)

10. NAIN—Where Jesus raised
the dead son of a widow
(See page 29)

11. BETH-ABARA—Where
John the Baptist preached
(See pages 14-16, 19)

12. CAESAREA PHILIPPI—
where Peter acknowl-
edged Jesus as
the Messiah
(See page 48)

SYRIA
PHOENICIA
GALILEE
CAESAREA PHILIPPI
BETHSAIDA
CAPERNAUM
CANA
NAZARETH
NAIN
SEA OF GALILEE
MEDITERRANEAN SEA
SAMARIA
SYCHAR
R. JORDAN
BETH-ABARA
PEREA
JERUSALEM
BETHLEHEM
DEAD SEA
JUDEA
ARABIA
N
E
S
W
EGYPT
Scale of Miles
0   10   20   30   40   50

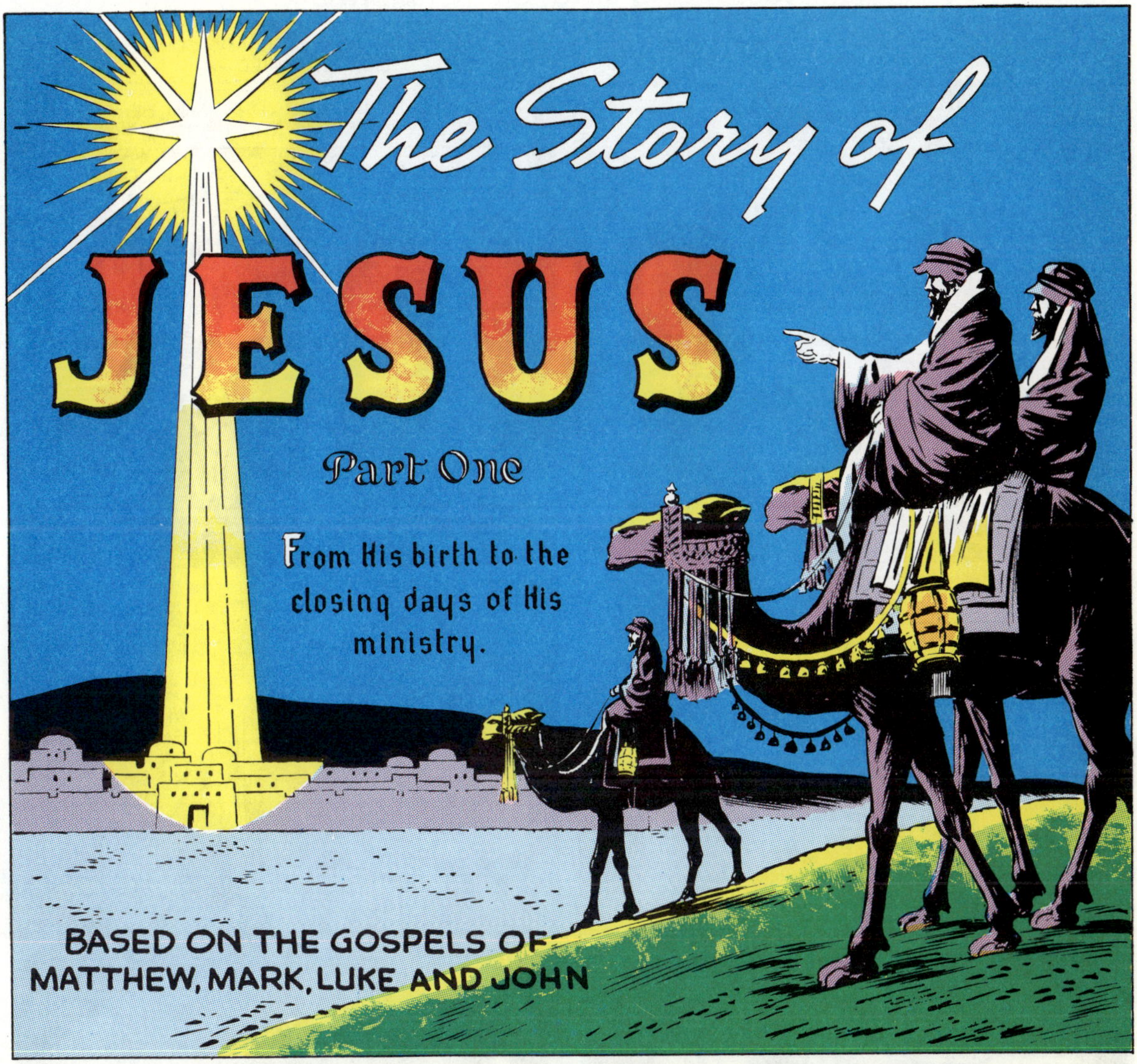

The Story of

JESUS

Part One

From His birth to the closing days of His ministry.

BASED ON THE GOSPELS OF MATTHEW, MARK, LUKE AND JOHN

Luke 1:1-38

LATER, MARY VISITED HER COUSIN ELIZABETH
YOU BRING TO ME JOY AND A SONG IN MY HEART, MARY. GOD HAS BEEN GOOD TO US BOTH!
I SHALL STAY AWHILE WITH YOU, ELIZABETH

AFTER A TIME, WHEN MARY WAS GONE, ELIZABETH BORE A CHILD ~~~
HE SHALL BE CALLED JOHN AND BE A PROPHET PREPARING THE PEOPLE FOR THE WAY OF THE LORD!
THE CHILD WHOM GOD'S ANGEL PROMISED! NOW AM I HAPPY!

NOW A TIME CAME WHEN ALL THE PEOPLE IN THE ROMAN EMPIRE WERE TO BE TAXED AFTER A CENSUS WAS TAKEN....

CAESAR AUGUSTUS COMMANDS EVERYONE TO RETURN TO HIS BIRTHPLACE TO REGISTER, AT ONCE!
WHEN THE EMPEROR COMMANDS-- WE MUST OBEY!

...AND SINCE GALILEE AND JUDEA WERE THEN PART OF THE ROMAN EMPIRE.....
MARY, WE MUST GO FROM OUR HOME IN NAZARETH TO REGISTER IN BETHLEHEM!
YES, JOSEPH, IT IS NOT LONG NOW BEFORE GOD WILL PRESENT US WITH THE PROMISED CHILD....SUPPOSE BETHLEHEM IS CROWDED!

AND BETHLEHEM WAS CROWDED ~~~
NOT A ROOM TO BE HAD—AND DARKNESS IS DUE!
THIS STABLE, JOSEPH, —IT WILL SERVE US ONE NIGHT—I SEE A MANGER IN IT!

AND THERE, JESUS WAS BORN, AND MARY WRAPPED HIM IN SWADDLING CLOTHES AND LAID HIM IN A MANGER ---

WE SHALL CALL HIM JESUS AS THE ANGEL TOLD US AND HE SHALL SAVE THE PEOPLE FROM THEIR SINS ---
MY SON!

DURING THE NIGHT - WHILE SHEPHERDS WERE KEEPING WATCH OVER THEIR FLOCKS ---
A STRANGE LIGHT COMES — WHAT IS IT?
IS A MIRACLE TO COME? — LOOK ---

AN ANGEL OF THE LORD APPEARS AS THEY CROWD ABOUT, FEARFUL ---
DO NOT BE AFRAID FOR I BRING YOU HAPPY NEWS! THIS DAY IN BETHLEHEM IS A SAVIOUR BORN, JESUS CHRIST THE LORD ---
LISTEN! THE TIME SPOKEN OF LONG AGO HAS COME!

AND SUDDENLY FROM HEAVEN VOICES WERE HEARD BY THE SHEPHERDS WHO LOOK UP ---
GLORY TO GOD IN THE HIGHEST AND ON EARTH PEACE TO MEN OF GOOD WILL

SEEK FOR THE STABLE OF AN INN — HE LIES IN A MANGER FOR A CRIB!
AT LAST — IT IS WHAT WE HAVE WAITED FOR AND WE SHALL WORSHIP HIM!

Matthew 2:1-6 Luke 2:16-20

HEROD SUMMONS THE WISE MEN ~~~
SEEK THIS BABE – AND BRING ME WORD, SO, I, TOO MAY HONOR HIM!
AS YOU COMMAND!

THE EASTERN STAR LEADS US AGAIN!
IT GOES BEFORE US —

GOLD AND FRANKINCENSE AND MYRRH, WE BRING YOU!
HE'S TRULY THE CHRIST CHILD!

THAT NIGHT ~~~
DO NOT RETURN TO KING HEROD AS HE PLANS HARM TO THE CHILD! – GO BACK HOME ANOTHER WAY!
WE OBEY!

WHEN THE WISE MEN DID NOT RETURN TO HEROD ~~~
ALL NIGHT I WAIT FOR THEM AND THEY HAVE GONE! – GET OUT THE SOLDIERS – SLAY ALL CHILDREN UP TO TWO YEARS OLD!
THIS IS A CRUEL ORDER!

BUT THE ANGEL APPEARS TO JOSEPH IN A DREAM ~~~
TAKE THE CHILD AND MARY AND FLEE TO EGYPT FOR HEROD PLANS TO SLAY HIM!

WE MUST HURRY, MARY! ALREADY THE SOLDIERS ARE CARRYING OUT THE ORDERS TO KILL THE CHILDREN OF BETHLEHEM!
GOD WILL GUIDE AND PROTECT US!

Matthew 2:15-23 Luke 2:39-42

WHEN JESUS WAS TWELVE HIS FATHER BELIEVED IT TIME TO TAKE HIM TO JERUSALEM TO GET THE FULL SIGNIFICANCE OF THEIR RELIGION.
JESUS WILL SEE JERUSALEM AND THE HOLY TEMPLE!
THIS WILL INDEED BE A DAY HE WON'T FORGET!

WHEN THE PASSOVER FEAST WAS OVER AND ALL STARTED FOR HOME.....
IS JESUS WITH YOU?
I THOUGHT HE WAS WITH YOU!

HAS ANYONE SEEN OUR SON JESUS?
WE'VE GONE A DAY'S JOURNEY AND HE'S NOT AMONG US!
WHY NOT GO BACK — HE'S PROBABLY STILL IN JERUSALEM!

THIRD DAY AFTER, THEY RETURN AND FIND HIM IN THE HOLY TEMPLE ~~~
HE IS HERE WITH THE WISE TEACHERS
JESUS — MY SON!

HE HAS BEEN ASKING AND ANSWERING QUESTIONS — HE ASTONISHES US!
WHY HAVE YOU DEALT WITH US THIS WAY, SON? WE HAVE SOUGHT YOU, SORROWING!

HOW IS IT YOU HAVE SOUGHT ME ELSEWHERE? — DID YOU NOT KNOW I MUST BE ABOUT MY FATHER'S BUSINESS?
WHAT MEANS MY BOY?

Luke 2:50-52, 3:1-23 Matthew 3:1-14. Mark 1:1-11

AFTER JESUS IS BAPTIZED BY JOHN HE IS DIRECTED BY THE HOLY SPIRIT TO GO INTO THE WILDERNESS — THERE HE PLANS THE KINGDOM OF GOD ON EARTH, FASTING FOR FORTY DAYS AND TEMPTED BY SATAN

JESUS IS TEMPTED TO USE HIS OWN POWER TO RELIEVE HIS HUNGER —

IF YOU ARE THE SON OF GOD COMMAND THAT THESE STONES BECOME LOAVES OF BREAD!

IT IS WRITTEN, MAN SHALL NOT LIVE BY BREAD ALONE BUT BY EVERY WORD OF GOD!

NEXT SATAN SUGGESTS THAT JESUS PERFORM A MIRACLE FROM A HIGH PINNACLE OF THE TEMPLE IN JERUSALEM BEFORE THE LARGE CROWDS GATHERED BELOW —

THROW YOURSELF DOWN, GOD'S ANGELS WILL BEAR YOU UP!

IT IS WRITTEN AGAIN, THOU SHALT NOT TEMPT THE LORD THY GOD!

THEN SATAN, ON TOP OF A MOUNTAIN, PROMISES GREAT REWARDS IF JESUS WILL SERVE HIM —

FROM HERE YOU SEE ALL THE KINGDOMS OF THE WORLD AND THE GLORY OF THEM — ALL THESE AND GREAT POWER WILL BE YOURS IF YOU WILL SERVE ME!

GET THEE BEHIND ME SATAN, FOR IT IS WRITTEN THOU SHALT WORSHIP THE LORD THY GOD AND HIM ONLY SHALT THOU SERVE!

THE TEMPTER, THUS DEFEATED, LEAVES JESUS AND, BEHOLD, ANGELS COME AND MINISTER TO HIM —

JESUS RETURNS TO WHERE JOHN IS BAPTIZING ---
BEHOLD THE LAMB OF GOD WHICH TAKES AWAY THE SIN OF THE WORLD-THIS IS HE OF WHOM I FORETOLD!

TWO OF JOHN THE BAPTIST'S DISCIPLES (ANOTHER JOHN AND ANDREW) FOLLOW AND TALK TO JESUS ---
MASTER WHERE DO YOU LIVE?
COME AND SEE!
WE GLADLY OBEY-WE WILL STAY WITH HIM AS LONG AS WE CAN

AFTER THE DAY'S VISIT OF JOHN AND ANDREW, ANDREW GOES TO SEEK HIS BROTHER SIMON ---
WE HAVE AT LAST FOUND THE MESSIAH CALLED THE CHRIST AND JOHN AND I HAVE BECOME HIS DISCIPLES!
TAKE ME TO HIM. I WOULD LIKE TO SEE HIM!

SIMON MEETS JESUS AND IS CALLED CEPHUS OR PETER-INTERPRETED MEANING A STONE
THOU ARE SIMON—THOU SHALT BE CALLED CEPHAS!
JESUS NOW HAS THREE DISCIPLES-JOHN, ANDREW AND PETER ---

JOHN AND PETER DECIDE AS DISCIPLES TO LEARN MORE ABOUT JESUS AND FOLLOW HIM ---
LET US GO INTO THE COUNTRY OF GALILEE, MASTER!
WE WILL DO YOUR BIDDING!
I TOO DESIRE TO FOLLOW THEE!

JESUS NEXT SECURES PHILIP AS A DISCIPLE ---
I LIVE IN BETHSAIDA, THE HOME OF ANDREW AND PETER!
FOLLOW ME!

PHILIP IS SO IMPRESSED WITH JESUS AS THE MESSIAH THAT HE SEEKS OUT NATHANAEL HIS FRIEND TO TELL HIM ---
WE HAVE FOUND HIM ABOUT WHOM MOSES IN THE LAW WROTE-JESUS OF NAZARETH, THE SON OF JOSEPH, COME AND SEE HIM!
CAN THERE ANY GOOD THING COME OUT OF NAZARETH?

NATHANAEL AFTER TALKING WITH JESUS IS CONVINCED THAT HE IS THE PROMISED MESSIAH — HE BECOMES A DISCIPLE ···
BEHOLD A TRUE ISRAELITE IN WHOM THERE IS NO GUILE — BEFORE PHILIP CALLED THEE, WHEN THOU WAST UNDER THE FIG TREE, I SAW THEE!
RABBI, THOU ART THE SON OF GOD··· THE KING OF ISRAEL!

AND THERE WAS A WEDDING FEAST IN CANA OF GALILEE — JESUS, HIS MOTHER AND HIS DISCIPLES WERE THERE ···
A TERRIBLE THING HAS HAPPENED — THERE IS NO MORE WINE FOR THE WEDDING — CAN YOUR SON JESUS HELP?
WHATSOEVER JESUS SAYS TO YOU — DO IT!
2

FILL THE WATERPOTS WITH WATER!
WHAT IS HE DOING?
3

WHAT'S UP? MORE WATER?
WE WISH WINE NOT WATER FOR THIS WEDDING FEAST!
WAIT — WATCH!

DRAW OUT NOW AND BEAR UNTO THE GOVERNOR OF THE FEAST!
IS THIS A MIRACLE?
5

THE GOVERNOR OF THE FEAST CALLS THE BRIDEGROOM AND CONGRATULATES HIM FOR HAVING SUCH GOOD WINE ···
WONDERFUL WINE! MOST HOSTS SERVE THE BEST WINE FIRST — YOU KEPT IT TO THE LAST!
IT IS WATER MADE WINE, — HE DOESNT KNOW IT!
IT IS A MIRACLE!
THIS FIRST RECORDED MIRACLE OF JESUS CONVINCES THE DISCIPLES OF JESUS' GREAT POWER
6

JESUS WITH HIS DISCIPLES VISITS JERUSALEM WHERE GREAT CROWDS ARE ATTENDING THE FEAST OF THE PASSOVER, THE GREAT ANNUAL JEWISH CELEBRATION
THIS PASSOVER CELEBRATION CERTAINLY BRINGS PEOPLE HERE FROM ALL OVER!
YES, AND A LOT OF GRAFTING TRADERS AND MONEY CHANGERS!

JESUS MAKES A WHIP FROM CORDS
THE MASTER IS ANGRY—THE MONEY CHANGERS DEFILE THE TEMPLE BY THEIR UNHOLY BUSINESS!
HUSH, WAIT!

TAKE THESE THINGS HENCE! MAKE NOT MY FATHER'S HOUSE A HOUSE OF MERCHANDISE
THEY ARE GETTING WHAT THEY DESERVE!

WE PAID TO HAVE A PLACE IN THIS TEMPLE!
BY WHAT AUTHORITY ARE YOU DOING THIS?
WE WILL GET YOU FOR THIS!

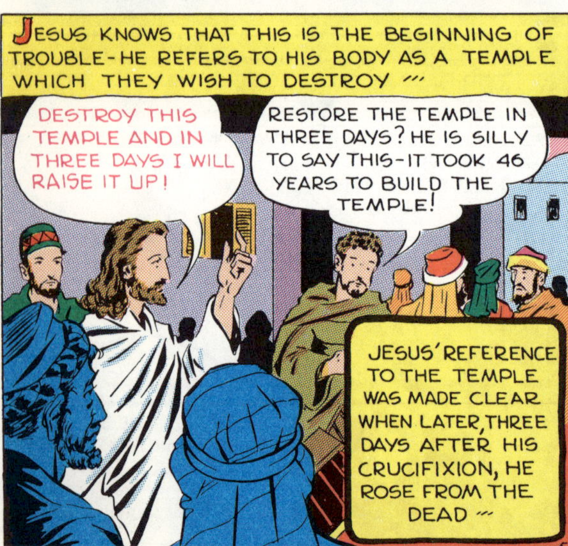
JESUS KNOWS THAT THIS IS THE BEGINNING OF TROUBLE—HE REFERS TO HIS BODY AS A TEMPLE WHICH THEY WISH TO DESTROY ⋯
DESTROY THIS TEMPLE AND IN THREE DAYS I WILL RAISE IT UP!
RESTORE THE TEMPLE IN THREE DAYS? HE IS SILLY TO SAY THIS—IT TOOK 46 YEARS TO BUILD THE TEMPLE!
JESUS' REFERENCE TO THE TEMPLE WAS MADE CLEAR WHEN LATER, THREE DAYS AFTER HIS CRUCIFIXION, HE ROSE FROM THE DEAD ⋯

A JEWISH RULER, NICODEMUS, LEARNING OF JESUS' MIRACLES IS ANXIOUS TO MEET HIM— HE COMES TO JESUS BY NIGHT ⋯
I'LL LEARN FOR MYSELF IF THIS JESUS IS THE PROMISED MESSIAH!

John 2:13-25

John 3:1-21, 3:25-30, 4:1-2

IN ORDER TO GET TO GALILEE, JESUS AND HIS DISCIPLES HAD TO TRAVEL THROUGH SAMARIA.
THIS IS THE CITY OF SYCHAR!
WE SHALL GO FIND FOOD, MASTER, WHILE YOU REST HERE
OVER YONDER IS JACOB'S WELL!

WHILE JESUS RESTS, A SAMARITAN WOMAN COMES TO DRAW WATER
GIVE ME TO DRINK!
HOW IS IT THAT YOU, A JEW, ASK A DRINK FROM A SAMARITAN, WITH WHOM THE JEWS HAVE NO DEALINGS!

IF THOU KNOWEST THE GIFT OF GOD AND WHO IT IS THAT SAYEST TO THEE, THOU WOULDST HAVE ASKED OF HIM AND HE WOULD HAVE GIVEN THEE LIVING WATER!
THE WELL IS DEEP— HOW WILL YOU GET THAT LIVING WATER? ARE YOU GREATER THAN OUR FATHER JACOB WHO GAVE US THE WELL!

WHOSOEVER DRINKETH THIS WATER SHALL THIRST AGAIN.... WHOSOEVER DRINKETH OF THE WATER THAT I SHALL GIVE...SHALL NEVER THIRST!
SIR, GIVE ME THIS WATER THAT I SHALL NOT THIRST...NEITHER COME SO FAR TO DRAW!

JESUS DISCLOSES TO THE WOMAN THAT HE IS THE MESSIAH....
I KNOW THAT WHEN THE MESSIAH WHO IS CALLED CHRIST COMES HE WILL TELL US ALL THINGS
I THAT SPEAK UNTO THEE, AM HE!

THE WOMAN IN HER EXCITEMENT LEAVES HER WATER PITCHER AT THE WELL AND GOES TO THE NEARBY CITY TELLING EVERYONE THAT SHE HAS MET THE MESSIAH ∼∼∼
WE KNOW INDEED YOU ARE THE CHRIST, THE SAVIOR OF THE WORLD!
NOW WE BELIEVE NOT BECAUSE OF WHAT THE WOMAN SAID, BUT, SINCE WE HAVE HEARD FOR OURSELVES!
WE WANT TO HEAR MORE, PLEASE STAY WITH US AWHILE!

John 4:2-42

AFTER TWO DAYS JESUS LEFT SAMARIA TO GO INTO GALILEE ....
THIS IS CANA WHERE YOU TURNED WATER INTO WINE!
WHO IS THIS NOBLEMAN RUNNING TO US!

PLEASE, MASTER, COME AND HEAL MY SON, HE IS DYING!
GO THY WAY, THY SON LIVETH!

THE NOBLEMAN, BELIEVING, HASTENS HOME ....
HOW IS MY SON .... JESUS SAID THAT HE WILL LIVE ....
MY LORD, COME QUICKLY A MIRACLE HAS HAPPENED!

SEE ....
MY SON LIVES! — JESUS WAS RIGHT!

YESTERDAY AT THE SEVENTH HOUR THE FEVER LEFT HIM!
IT WAS AT THAT SAME HOUR THAT JESUS TOLD ME TO GO HOME AND THAT MY SON WOULD LIVE!

JESUS RETURNS TO HIS BOYHOOD TOWN OF NAZARETH AND AS WAS HIS CUSTOM WENT INTO THE SYNAGOGUE ON THE SABBATH DAY ....
THIS IS THE BOOK OF THE PROPHET ISAIAH!

Luke 4:14-31 Matthew 4:13-16

MASTER— USE MY BOAT FROM WHICH YOU CAN TALK TO THE CROWD!
AT THE SEA OF GALILEE JESUS MEETS UP AGAIN WITH TWO OF HIS EARLY BELIEVERS, SIMON PETER AND HIS BROTHER ANDREW ╌╌
1

JESUS, AFTER SPEAKING TO A LARGE CROWD ON THE SHORE, PERFORMS A WONDERFUL MIRACLE ╌╌
SIMON LAUNCH DOWN INTO THE DEEP AND LET DOWN YOUR NETS FOR A DRAUGHT!
MASTER, WE HAVE FISHED ALL THE NIGHT AND TAKEN NOTHING, NEVERTHELESS, AT YOUR WORD I WILL LET DOWN THE NET!
2

SO GREAT WAS THE CATCH THAT SIMON PETER AND ANDREW CALLED FOR HELP TO THEIR PARTNERS JAMES AND JOHN IN ANOTHER BOAT ╌╌
DEPART FROM ME FOR I AM A SINFUL MAN, O LORD!
COME YE AFTER ME AND I WILL MAKE YOU TO BECOME FISHERS OF MEN!
WE ARE ALL CONVINCED. WE WILL BE YOUR DISCIPLES!
3

JESUS CURES A MAN IN A SYNAGOGUE WHO ACTS AS THOUGH HE WERE CRAZY
LET US ALONE— ARE YOU COME TO DESTROY US … HOLY ONE OF GOD?
HOLD THY PEACE AND COME OUT OF HIM!
WHAT A MAN! EVEN THE UNCLEAN SPIRITS OBEY HIM!
HE IS BECOMING FAMOUS FOR CURING PEOPLE!

JESUS, UPON LEAVING THE SYNAGOGUE, DECIDES TO GO TO PETER'S HOUSE IN CAPERNAUM…
MY WIFE'S MOTHER IS ILL, MASTER, SICK WITH A FEVER— CAN YOU NOT HEAL HER?

SHE RISES— SHE IS WELL AT YOUR TOUCH, LORD!
I'M VERY GRATEFUL— LET ME SERVE YOU NOW!
6

JESUS, AFTER A BUSY DAY OF HEALING, GOES INTO A DESERT PLACE BUT EVEN HERE PEOPLE FLOCK TO HIM ....
PLEASE STAY WITH US!
I MUST PREACH THE KINGDOM OF GOD TO OTHER CITIES, ALSO, FOR THEREFORE AM I SENT!

MASTER, IF YOU WILL, YOU CAN MAKE ME CLEAN!
LOOK-- JESUS TOUCHES THE LEPER!
ONE DAY A LEPER SOUGHT OUT JESUS

JESUS CURES THE LEPER AND ASKS HIM TO TELL NO ONE—BUT THE LEPER IS TOO HAPPY TO KEEP QUIET!
SAY NOTHING TO ANY MAN. GO AND OFFER FOR THY CLEANSING THOSE THINGS WHICH MOSES COMMANDED!
WHO HAS EVER CURED A LEPER BEFORE!

AND IN CAPERNAUM, LIVED A MAN WHO WAS PARALYZED ....
HERE COMES THAT PARALYZED MAN WITH FOUR FRIENDS CARRYING HIM!
THEY ARE NOT GOING TO GET HIM IN!

WE CANNOT GET NEAR, LET'S GO TO THE ROOF AND LET HIM DOWN!
AN EXCELLENT IDEA!

JESUS REWARDS THE FAITH AND THE PERSISTENCE OF THE FOUR FRIENDS ....
MAN, THY SINS BE FORGIVEN THEE.... ARISE AND TAKE UP THY COUCH AND GO INTO THINE HOUSE!
WHO CAN FORGIVE SIN EXCEPT GOD?
THIS IS WONDERFUL – IF HE CAN CURE A MAN, MAYBE, HE CAN FOR- GIVE SIN TOO!
AND IMMEDIATELY HE ROSE UP.... AND DEPARTED TO HIS OWN HOUSE, GLORIFYING GOD ....

JESUS CALLED MATTHEW (ALSO NAMED LEVI), THE TAX-GATHERER AT CAPERNAUM ...
STRANGE THINGS THAT THIS JESUS IS DOING...WHAT WORKS WILL HE DO HERE?
LOOK, HE SPEAKS TO LEVI THE PUBLICAN!

MASTER, I AM HONORED—HOW CAN I LEARN MORE OF YOUR TEACHINGS?
FOLLOW ME!
LOOK—MATTHEW IS CALLED TO BE HIS DISCIPLE TOO!
WONDER IF JESUS KNOWS HOW WE FEEL ABOUT LEVI!

MATTHEW IS SO HAPPY TO BE RECOGNIZED AS A DISCIPLE THAT HE MAKES A GREAT FEAST IN JESUS' HONOR ...
WHY DOES JESUS EAT AND DRINK WITH PUBLICANS AND SINNERS?
THEY THAT ARE WHOLE NEED NOT A PHYSICIAN BUT THEY THAT ARE SICK!

CERTAIN MEMBERS OF A RELIGIOUS SECT CALLED THE PHARISEES, OBJECT AS JESUS GOES THROUGH A WHEAT FIELD ON THE SABBATH DAY.....
IT IS NOT LAWFUL TO PICK GRAIN ON THE SABBATH!
WHY DO YOUR DISCIPLES DO WHAT IS NOT LAWFUL ON THE SABBATH DAY?
HAVE YOU NOT READ WHAT DAVID DID---WHEN...HUNGERED HE AND THEY WITH HIM...IN THE HOUSE OF GOD...ATE SHEW-BREAD?

THESE PHARISEES ARE ANGRY!
THE SABBATH WAS MADE FOR MAN AND NOT MAN FOR THE SABBATH—THEREFORE THE SON OF MAN IS LORD ALSO OF THE SABBATH!
JESUS IS BREAKING ALL OUR TRADITIONS!

JESUS GOES TO JERUSALEM —HE PASSES BY THE POOL OF BETHESDA...
MASTER... THE POOL IS CROWDED AT THIS TIME BECAUSE OF THE FEAST!
SEE-THIS PLACE IS FILLED WITH THE SICK HALT AND BLIND!

PEOPLE BELIEVED THAT WHEN THE WATER MOVED ABOUT, IT WAS BECAUSE OF AN ANGEL, AND THAT THE FIRST SICK PERSON STEPPING IN, WOULD THEN BE HEALED....
WILT THOU BE MADE WHOLE?
I'VE NO ONE TO PUT ME IN THE POOL WHEN IT MOVES—OTHERS GET AHEAD OF ME!

RISE—TAKE UP THY BED AND WALK!

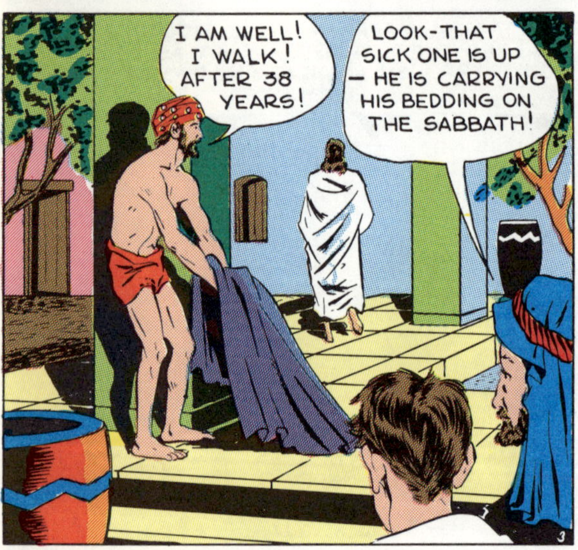
I AM WELL! I WALK! AFTER 38 YEARS!
LOOK—THAT SICK ONE IS UP—HE IS CARRYING HIS BEDDING ON THE SABBATH!

IT IS THE SABBATH AND NOT LAWFUL TO WORK ON THE SABBATH——
HE THAT MADE ME WHOLE TOLD ME TO CARRY THE BEDDING

THEY SEEK JESUS TO QUESTION HIM....
WHAT AUTHORITY GIVES YOU THE RIGHT TO TELL A MAN TO WORK ON THE SABBATH?
MY FATHER WORKETH AND I WORK—THE SON CAN DO NOTHING OF HIMSELF, BUT, WHAT THINGS HE SEETH THE FATHER DOETH—THESE ALSO DOETH THE SON LIKEWISE!

THE OPPOSITION AGAINST JESUS INCREASES....
WE'LL STOP HIM YET——HE IS BREAKING OUR SABBATH!
YES AND HE CALLS HIMSELF THE SON OF GOD!
THAT MAKES HIM EQUAL TO GOD—

John 5:1-47

Matthew 4:18-22, 10:2-4 Luke 6:12-16 Mark 1:16-20, 3:13-19

.... AND SEEING THE MULTITUDE, JESUS WENT UP INTO A MOUNTAIN AND TAUGHT THE PEOPLE SAYING:
BLESSED ARE THE POOR IN SPIRIT FOR THEIRS IS THE KINGDOM OF HEAVEN!
WHAT DOES 'BLESSED' MEAN?
IT MEANS BEING TRULY HAPPY WITHIN!
THIS ALSO MAKES HEAVEN WITHIN—NOT ABOVE IN SOME PLACE IN THE SKIES!

BLESSED ARE THEY THAT MOURN FOR THEY SHALL BE COMFORTED!
HIS WORDS ARE SO COMFORTING, I FEEL I CAN BEAR MY TROUBLES NOW!

BLESSED ARE THE MEEK FOR THEY SHALL INHERIT THE EARTH—THEY THAT HUNGER AND THIRST AFTER RIGHTEOUSNESS SHALL BE FILLED!
WISH THE ROMAN SOLDIERS, WHO THINK THEY ARE THE BIG SHOTS, COULD HEAR THIS!
JESUS SAYS IF WE CONTINUALLY SEEK GOODNESS SOME TIME WE WILL BE SATISFIED!

.....THE MERCIFUL SHALL OBTAIN MERCY··· THE PURE IN HEART SHALL SEE GOD!
THAT MEANS WE GET WHAT WE GIVE!
GOD SEEMS SO NEAR AS HE SPEAKS!

THE PEACEMAKERS SHALL BE CALLED THE CHILDREN OF GOD — THE PERSECUTED FOR RIGHTEOUSNESS' SAKE — THEIRS IS THE KINGDOM OF GOD
A QUEER IDEA THAT IF WE WORK FOR PEACE WE ARE THEN CALLED CHILDREN OF GOD!
HE SAYS IF PEOPLE SPEAK FALSELY AND PERSECUTE US UNJUSTLY WE SHOULD REJOICE!
IF WE ARE PERSECUTED FOR BELIEVING IN JESUS WE SHOULD BE GLAD!

JESUS PRAISES THOSE WHO ARE ACCEPTING HIS TEACHINGS"
YE ARE THE SALT OF THE EARTH— YE ARE THE LIGHT OF THE WORLD!
TO TELL OTHERS IS TO SPREAD HIS TEACHINGS!

A SAYING REMEMBERED BY PEOPLE THEN, AND BY MANY TODAY ···
LET YOUR LIGHT SO SHINE BEFORE MEN THAT THEY MAY SEE YOUR GOOD WORKS AND GLORIFY YOUR FATHER WHICH IS IN HEAVEN!

A SERVANT OF A ROMAN CENTURION IS DYING IN CAPERNAUM
GO TO JESUS WHO IS HEALING OTHERS — ASK HIM TO CURE MY DEVOTED SERVANT!
YOU HAVE BEEN GOOD TO OUR NATION — TO DO AS YOU ASK IS VERY LITTLE!

THE CENTURION'S FRIENDS COME TO JESUS AS HE AND HIS DISCIPLES ARE ENTERING CAPERNAUM
OUR ROMAN FRIEND, A WORTHY MAN, WHO BUILT US A SYNAGOGUE HAS A DYING SERVANT — WILL YOU COME?
I WILL COME AND HEAL HIM!

THE CENTURION SHOWS HIS FAITH IN JESUS' POWER TO HEAL
I AM NOT WORTHY TO HAVE YOU COME UNDER MY ROOF BUT SPEAK THE WORD ONLY AND I KNOW MY SERVANT SHALL BE HEALED!
HE THINKS JESUS CAN COMMAND SICKNESS TO DEPART JUST LIKE THE CENTURION ORDERS HIS SOLDIERS TO GO OR TO COME!
I SAY UNTO YOU I HAVE NOT FOUND SUCH GREAT FAITH, NO, NOT IN ALL ISRAEL!
AND HIS SICK SERVANT WAS FOUND INSIDE THE HOUSE, ENTIRELY CURED.

JESUS AND HIS DISCIPLES WITH CROWDS FOLLOWING APPROACH THE CITY OF NAIN
A FUNERAL PROCESSION, MASTER!
YES, THIS WIDOW OF NAIN HAS LOST HER ONLY SON!

WEEP NOT — — WOMAN . . . . I SAY UNTO THEE, YOUNG MAN, ARISE!

HE IS ALIVE!
MOTHER, I AM WELL!
A GREAT PROPHET IS AMONG US!
GOD HAS VISITED HIS PEOPLE!

Matthew 11:2-19   Luke 3:19-20, 7:18-50

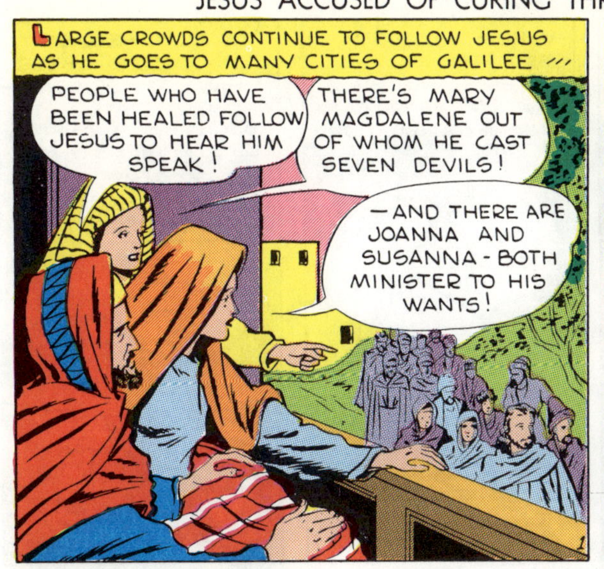

Matthew 12:22-50 Mark 3:22-35 Luke 8:2-3, 11:14-26

"THE SEED ON THE STONY GROUND ARE THEY WHO, WHEN THEY RECEIVE THE WORD, IMMEDIATELY RECEIVE IT WITH GLADNESS AND HAVE NO ROOT IN THEMSELVES AND SO ENDURE BUT FOR A TIME. AFTERWARDS WHEN AFFLICTION OR PERSECUTION ARISES FOR THE WORD'S SAKE, IMMEDIATELY, THEY ARE OFFENDED" ~

"THOSE SOWN AMONG THE THORNS HEAR THE WORD, AND THE CARES OF THIS WORLD AND THE DECEITFULNESS OF RICHES AND THE LUSTS OF OTHER THINGS ENTERING IN CHOKE THE WORD, AND IT BECOMETH UNFRUITFUL." ~

"THOSE SOWN ON GOOD GROUND RECEIVE IT AND BRING FORTH FRUIT SOME THIRTY FOLD, SOME SIXTY AND SOME ONE HUNDRED FOLD."

Matthew 13:1-23 Mark 4:1-20 Luke 8:4-15

JESUS EXPLAINS OTHER PARABLES TO HIS DISCIPLES ···
EXPLAIN THE OTHER PARABLES!
YES, TELL US ABOUT THE SOWER OF WHEAT AND THE WEEDS ON HIS FARM!
THE KINGDOM OF HEAVEN····

"· IS LIKE··· A MAN WHO SOWED GOOD SEED IN HIS FIELD "

"AND WHILE MEN SLEPT HIS ENEMY CAME AND SOWED WEEDS AMONG THE WHEAT "

SIR, DIDN'T YOU SOW GOOD SEED? WHERE THEN HAVE THESE WEEDS COME FROM?
SHALL WE PULL THEM UP?
LET THEM BOTH GROW TOGETHER UNTIL THE HARVEST. THEN THE REAPERS WILL GATHER AND BIND UP THE WEEDS AND BURN THEM, BUT WILL GATHER THE WHEAT INTO MY BARNS!

THE FIELD IS THE WORLD—THE GOOD SEED ARE CHILDREN OF THE KINGDOM, —WEEDS THE CHILDREN OF THE WICKED— THE ENEMY, THE DEVIL, THE HARVEST— THE END OF THE WORLD. REAPERS—THE ANGELS, AS THE WEEDS ARE GATHERED AND BURNED, SO SHALL IT BE AT THE END OF THE WORLD—THEN SHALL THE RIGHTEOUS SHINE FORTH AS THE SUN IN THE KINGDOM OF THEIR FATHER!

THE KINGDOM OF HEAVEN IS LIKE····

"····A GRAIN OF MUSTARD SEED WHICH A MAN SOWS IN HIS FIELD.

"THIS INDEED IS THE SMALLEST OF ALL SEEDS, BUT WHEN IT GROWS UP IT IS LARGER THAN ANY HERB AND BECOMES A TREE, SO THAT THE BIRDS OF THE AIR COME AND DWELL IN ITS BRANCHES "

Matthew 13:44-52

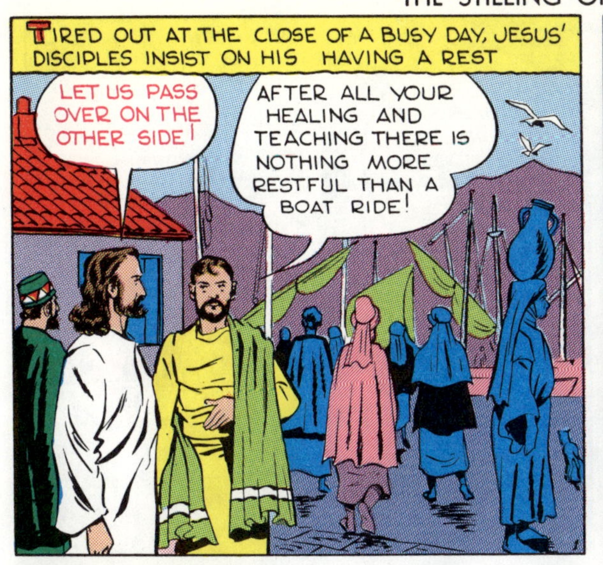

Matthew 8:23-34 Mark 4:35-41, 5:1-19 Luke 8:22-39

Matthew 9:18-26 Mark 5:21-43 Luke 8:41-56

TWO BLIND MEN ASK TO BE HEALED
THESE TWO BLIND MEN HAVE FOLLOWED US INTO THE HOUSE!
THOU SON OF DAVID HAVE PITY ON US!
BELIEVE YE THAT I AM ABLE TO DO THIS?
YES, LORD!

JESUS CURES THEIR BLINDNESS ~
ACCORDING TO YOUR FAITH BE IT UNTO YOU!
I SEE!
THANK GOD! SO DO I!

JESUS ON HIS THIRD YEAR OF MINISTRY RETURNS TO HIS HOME TOWN OF NAZARETH WHERE HE IS REJECTED THE SECOND TIME ~~
WHERE HAS THIS MAN LEARNED TO DO THESE THINGS?
HE IS THE CARPENTER WHO LIVED HERE — THE SON OF MARY. I KNOW HIS BROTHERS, JAMES, JOSES SIMON AND JUDAH, ALSO HIS SISTERS!
A PROPHET IS NOT WITHOUT HONOR BUT IN HIS OWN COUNTRY AND AMONG HIS OWN KIN AND IN HIS OWN HOUSE!

IN NAZARETH BECAUSE OF THE PEOPLE'S UNBELIEF HE WAS UNABLE TO DO ANY GREAT WORK
JESUS IS GRIEVED BECAUSE SO MANY DO NOT HAVE CONFIDENCE IN HIM!

JESUS GOES ABOUT IN THE CITIES AND VILLAGES, TEACHING IN THE SYNAGOGUES, PREACHING AND HEALING PEOPLE OF EVERY DISEASE ~~
THE HARVEST TRULY IS PLENTEOUS, THE LABORERS FEW — PRAY THAT THE LORD OF THE HARVEST SEND FORTH LABORERS!
YES, LORD, — THERE IS SO MUCH TO DO!
ALL YOUR DISCIPLES WILL BE GLAD TO HELP YOU!

JESUS CALLS HIS TWELVE DISCIPLES TOGETHER — HE INSTRUCTS AND GIVES THEM POWER TO CARRY ON HIS MISSION ~~
GO PREACH, THE KINGDOM OF HEAVEN IS AT HAND, HEAL THE SICK, CLEANSE THE LEPERS, RAISE THE DEAD, CAST OUT DEVILS!
WE WILL GO AS SHEEP AMONG WOLVES FOR MANY WILL REJECT US AS THEY DID YOU!
WE'LL NOT BE AFRAID! WE'LL HAVE, AS YOU SAY, THE SPIRIT OF OUR HEAVENLY FATHER WITH US!

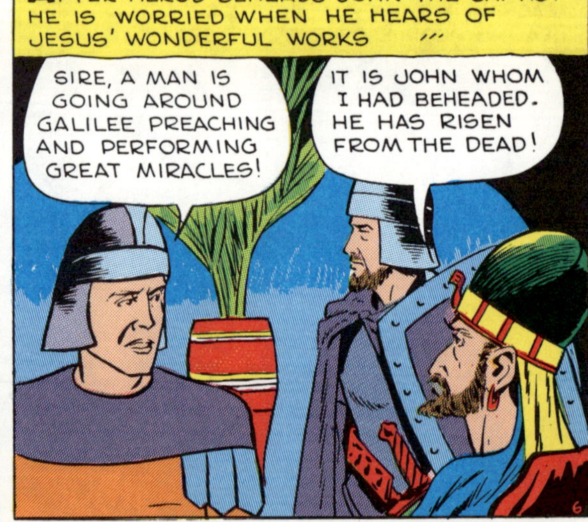

Matthew 10:1, 14:1-12 Mark 6:7-29 Luke 9:1-9

THE FEEDING OF THE FIVE THOUSAND

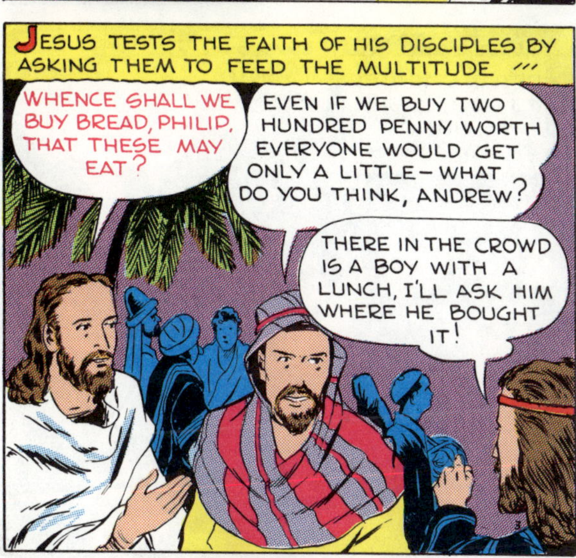

Matthew 14:13-21 Mark 6:30-46 Luke 9:10-17 John 6:1-14

IN ORDER THAT HE BE ALONE FOR PRAYER — HE SENDS THE MULTITUDE AWAY AND ASKS HIS DISCIPLES TO SAIL AROUND THE TURN IN THE LAKE, WHERE HE WILL JOIN THEM.

JESUS, FROM THE SHORE, SEES THE DISCIPLES IN A SEVERE STORM MAKING LITTLE HEADWAY IN THEIR ROWING
WE'RE NOT GETTING VERY FAR IN THIS STORM!
WISH JESUS WERE WITH US AGAIN TO CALM THIS TEMPEST!

SUDDENLY THE DISCIPLES ARE AWED TO SEE A SPIRIT-LIKE FORM WALKING ON THE WATER
LOOK, SEE THE SPIRIT ON THE WATER!
DID YOU EVER SEE ANYTHING LIKE IT, PETER?
BE OF GOOD CHEER, IT IS I, BE NOT AFRAID'
LORD, IF IT IS YOU, LET ME COME TO YOU ON THE WATER!

PETER ATTEMPTS TO GO TO JESUS WALKING ON THE WATER —
LORD SAVE ME! — I'M SINKING!
O, THOU OF LITTLE FAITH, WHEREFORE DOST THOU DOUBT —

WHEN THEY WERE COME INTO THE SHIP THE WIND CEASED
YOU ARE TRULY THE SON OF GOD!

WHEN JESUS LEFT THE BOAT ON THE OTHER SIDE PEOPLE WERE THERE AGAIN BRINGING THEIR SICK
OH, MASTER CURE MY POOR BOY!
CURE MY BLINDNESS, MASTER!
IF I JUST TOUCH THE BORDER OF HIS GARMENT I'LL BE HEALED!

THE PEOPLE WHO HAD SEEN JESUS FEED THE MULTITUDE FOLLOW HIM BY BOAT TO CAPERNAUM
HOW DID HE GET OVER HERE?
WE SAW HIS DISCIPLES LEAVE, BUT NOT JESUS!
OUR FOREFATHERS ESCAPING FROM EGYPT WERE GIVEN MANNA AS BREAD FROM HEAVEN, BY MOSES OUR LEADER!
YE SEEK ME… BECAUSE YE DID EAT OF THE LOAVES AND WERE FILLED…. LABOUR NOT FOR THE MEAT WHICH PERISHETH BUT FOR THE MEAT WHICH ENDURETH UNTO EVERLASTING LIFE, WHICH THE SON OF MAN SHALL GIVE UNTO YOU!

MOSES GAVE YOU NOT THAT BREAD FROM HEAVEN— MY FATHER GIVETH YOU THE TRUE BREAD FROM HEAVEN!
THEY ARE LOOKING FOR ANOTHER MIRACULOUS FEEDING!

I CAME TO DO THE WILL OF HIM WHO SENT ME— EVERYONE WHO SEETH THE SON AND BELIEVETH IN HIM SHALL HAVE EVERLASTING LIFE!
IS NOT THIS JESUS THE SON OF JOSEPH WHOSE FATHER AND MOTHER WE KNOW?

I AM THE LIVING BREAD—IF ANY MAN EAT HE WILL LIVE FOREVER—THE BREAD THAT I WILL GIVE IS MY FLESH!
HOW CAN THIS MAN GIVE US HIS FLESH TO EAT!
IT IS TOO HARD FOR ME TO BELIEVE —LET'S GET OUT OF HERE WITH SUCH FOOLISH TALK!

WHEN JESUS WAS ALONE WITH HIS DISCIPLES HE EXPLAINED WHAT HE MEANT …
THE FLESH PROFITETH NOTHING. —THE WORDS THAT I SPEAK… ARE SPIRIT AND THEY ARE LIFE… WILL YE ALSO GO AWAY?
SPEAK UP PETER AND ANSWER!
LORD TO WHOM SHALL WE GO— THOU HAST THE WORDS OF ETERNAL LIFE— WE ARE SURE THAT YOU ARE THAT CHRIST THE SON OF THE LIVING GOD!

HAVE I NOT CHOSEN YOU TWELVE AND ONE OF YOU IS A DEVIL!
JESUS WAS SPEAKING OF JUDAS ISCARIOT WHO LATER BETRAYED HIM…

Matthew 15:1-20 Mark 7:1-23

ALONG THE COAST CITIES OF TYRE AND SIDON WHERE JESUS AND HIS DISCIPLES GO TO GET REST, LIVES A CANAANITE WOMAN WITH A SICK DAUGHTER.
THE GREAT JEWISH DOCTOR WHO HAS CURED OTHERS CAN CURE YOUR LITTLE GIRL!
YES, I KNOW HE CAN—THERE HE IS APPROACHING I WILL PLEAD WITH HIM!

JESUS MAKES NO REPLY TO THE MOTHER'S PLEADING
HAVE MERCY ON ME, OH LORD! MY LITTLE DAUGHTER IS GRIEVOUSLY VEXED WITH A DEVIL!
THIS GENTILE WOMAN IS BOTHERING JESUS!

CONTRARY TO JESUS' USUAL RESPONSE FOR HELP HE SEEMS TO DENY THIS WOMAN'S REQUEST
SEND HER AWAY FOR SHE HAS BEEN CRYING AFTER US!
I AM NOT SENT BUT TO THE LOST SHEEP OF THE HOUSE OF ISRAEL!
WE HAVE ENOUGH TO DO WITHOUT BEING BOTHERED BY HER!

THE MOTHER PERSISTS IN HER PLEAS FOR HER LITTLE GIRL
IT IS NOT MEET TO TAKE THE CHILDREN'S BREAD AND TO CAST IT TO THE DOGS!
IT IS TRUE, MASTER, YET THE LITTLE DOGS UNDER THE TABLE EAT THE CRUMBS FROM THE MASTER'S TABLE!

GO, WOMAN GREAT IS THY FAITH, BE IT UNTO THEE EVEN AS THOU WILT!

MOTHER FINDS DAUGHTER AS JESUS HAD STATED, CURED, FROM THE TIME HE HAD SPOKEN
MOTHER, I KNOW I AM CURED NOW!
MY DAUGHTER!

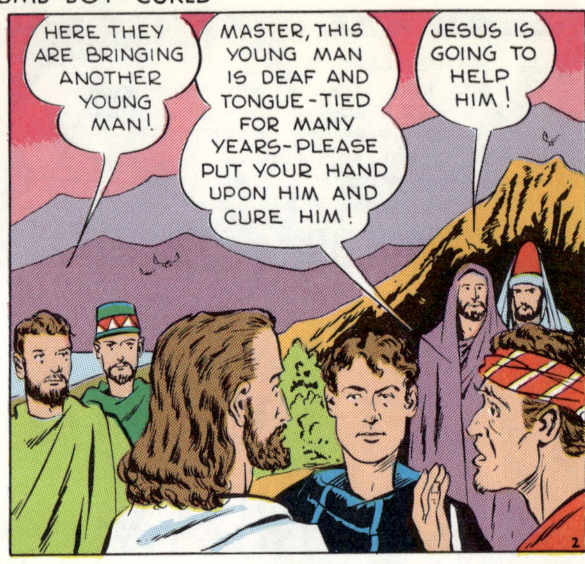

Matthew 15:29-31 Mark 7:31-37

Matthew 15:32-39 Mark 8:1-10

WHEN JESUS HAD GONE BY SHIP TO CAPERNAUM ON THE OTHER SIDE OF THE LAKE, A GROUP OF PHARISEES AND SADDUCEES (ANOTHER RELIGIOUS SECT) COME TO TRIP HIM WITH QUESTIONS.
WE HAVE HEARD OF YOUR MIRACLES- SHOW US A SIGN FROM HEAVEN!
WHEN IT IS EVENING, YE SAY IT WILL BE FAIR WEATHER, FOR THE SKY IS RED- AND LOWERING·O YE HYPOCRITES, YE CAN DISCERN THE FACE OF THE SKY, BUT CAN YE NOT DISCERN THE SIGNS OF THE TIMES?

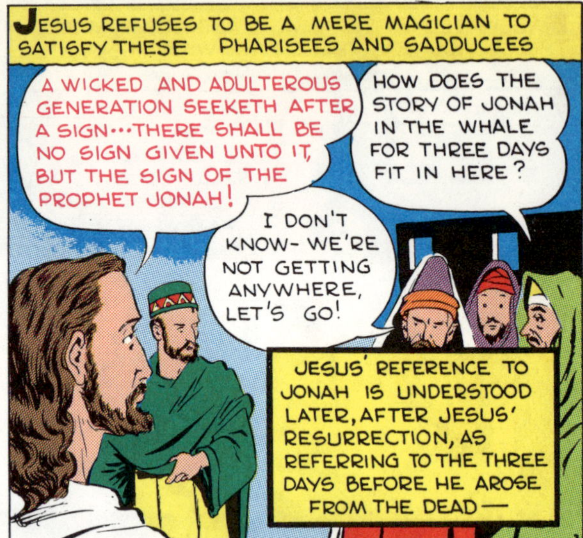
JESUS REFUSES TO BE A MERE MAGICIAN TO SATISFY THESE PHARISEES AND SADDUCEES
A WICKED AND ADULTEROUS GENERATION SEEKETH AFTER A SIGN···THERE SHALL BE NO SIGN GIVEN UNTO IT, BUT THE SIGN OF THE PROPHET JONAH!
HOW DOES THE STORY OF JONAH IN THE WHALE FOR THREE DAYS FIT IN HERE?
I DON'T KNOW- WE'RE NOT GETTING ANYWHERE, LET'S GO!
JESUS' REFERENCE TO JONAH IS UNDERSTOOD LATER, AFTER JESUS' RESURRECTION, AS REFERRING TO THE THREE DAYS BEFORE HE AROSE FROM THE DEAD —

WHEN JESUS AND HIS DISCIPLES COME TO THE OTHER SIDE OF THE LAKE, THEY HAD FORGOTTEN TO TAKE FOOD ~·
WE LEFT IN SUCH A HURRY WE FORGOT TO TAKE BREAD WITH US!
I HAVE ONE LOAF – THAT'S NOT ENOUGH!

TAKE HEED AND BEWARE OF THE LEAVEN OF THE PHARISEES AND SADDUCEES!
IT IS BECAUSE WE HAVE TAKEN NO BREAD THAT HE IS SAYING THIS!
NO, I DON'T THINK THAT IS WHAT HE MEANS!

O YE OF LITTLE FAITH! WHY REASON YE AMONG YOURSELVES BECAUSE YE HAVE BROUGHT NO BREAD– REMEMBER THE FIVE LOAVES AND THE FIVE THOUSAND AND THE SEVEN LOAVES AND THE FOUR THOUSAND!
WE CERTAINLY OUGHT NOT TO WORRY ABOUT LACK OF FOOD –JESUS ALWAYS MEETS ALL OUR NEEDS!

YE DO NOT UNDERSTAND···I SPAKE NOT CONCERNING BREAD,– BUT THAT YE SHOULD BEWARE OF THE LEAVEN OF THE PHARISEES AND THE SADDUCEES!
HE IS WARNING ABOUT FALSE TEACHINGS WHICH HE CALLS LEAVEN!
YES, THEY INSIST ON A LOT OF FORM, BUT THEIR HEARTS ARE FAR FROM GOD!

IN BETHSAIDA JESUS WAS ASKED TO CURE A YOUNG BLIND MAN
PLEASE, MASTER, TOUCH THE EYES OF MY FRIEND AND CURE HIM!
THIS TOWN IS NOT THE PLACE WHERE JESUS WILL HEAL HIM!

JESUS TAKES THE BLIND MAN AND LEADS HIM OUT OF THE TOWN
JESUS SEEMS TO BE PRESSING HIS LIPS AGAINST THE MAN'S EYES!
THIS IS A DIFFICULT CASE TO CURE!

JESUS' METHOD APPEARS TO BE ONLY PARTIALLY SUCCESSFUL
JESUS ASKS HIM IF HE CAN SEE ANYTHING!
AS I LOOK UP I SEE INDISTINCTLY MEN AS TREES WALKING!

ANOTHER TOUCH AND THE MAN SEES
JESUS WILL NOT BE SATISFIED UNTIL HIS VISION IS COMPLETELY RESTORED!
JESUS ASKS HIM AGAIN IF HE CAN SEE BETTER!
PRAISE GOD I SEE EVERY MAN NOW VERY CLEARLY!

FOR SOME REASON JESUS DOES NOT WANT THE PEOPLE OF THE TOWN TO KNOW OF HIS CURES
NEITHER GO INTO THE TOWN NOR TELL TO ANY IN THE TOWN!

YOU HAVE BROUGHT JOY TO ANOTHER YOUNG MAN!

Mark 8:22-26

JESUS AND HIS DISCIPLES GO TO THE COAST OF CAESAREA PHILIPPI ~~
WHO DO MEN SAY THAT I AM?
SOME SAY YOU ARE JOHN THE BAPTIST!
SOME SAY YOU ARE ELIJAH, OTHERS SAY JEREMIAH OR ONE OF THE PROPHETS!

JESUS LEARNS HOW HIS DISCIPLES FEEL TOWARDS HIM, AS PETER CONFESSES THAT HE REGARDS HIM AS THE MESSIAH.
BUT WHO SAY YE THAT I AM?
THOU ART THE CHRIST, THE SON OF THE LIVING GOD!

PETER'S ACKNOWLEDGEMENT OF JESUS AS THE CHRIST, BRINGS A MOST IMPORTANT STATEMENT FROM JESUS.
BLESSED ART THOU SIMON BAR-JONA, FLESH AND BLOOD HATH NOT REVEALED IT UNTO THEE BUT MY FATHER WHO IS IN HEAVEN!

JESUS INDICATES THAT THE KINGDOM OF GOD IS BUILT UPON THE ROCK OF "FAITH IN HIM"
....THOU ART PETER AND UPON THIS ROCK I WILL BUILD MY CHURCH~ AND THE GATES OF HELL SHALL NOT PREVAIL AGAINST IT!

I WILL GIVE UNTO THEE THE KEYS OF THE KINGDOM OF HEAVEN AND WHATSOEVER THOU SHALT BIND ON EARTH SHALL BE BOUND IN HEAVEN AND WHATSOEVER THOU SHALT LOOSE ON EARTH SHALL BE LOOSED IN HEAVEN!

ALTHOUGH JESUS HAD REVEALED TO THE SAMARITAN WOMAN THAT HE WAS THE MESSIAH, HE NOW FEELS THAT OTHERS ARE NOT YET PREPARED TO KNOW THIS.
WHAT A WONDERFUL RESPONSIBILITY HE IS GIVING TO US!
JESUS EXPECTS US TO PASS ALONG THESE GREAT TRUTHS!
TELL NO MAN THAT I AM JESUS THE CHRIST!

Matthew 16:21-28 Mark 8:31-38 Luke 9:22-27

Matthew 17:1-13 Mark 9:2-13 Luke 9:28-36

Matthew 17:14-21 Mark 9:14-29 Luke 9:37-42

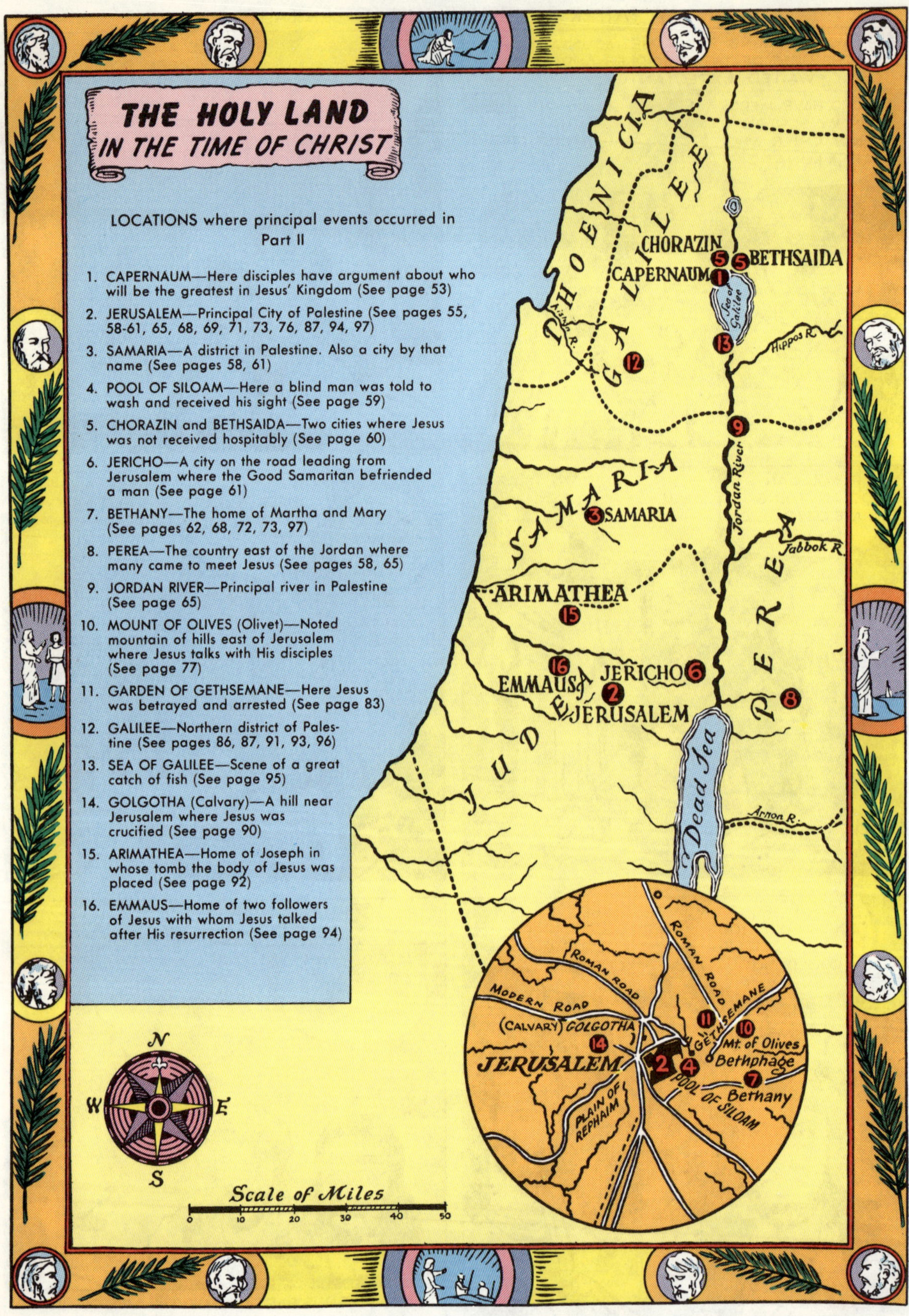

THE HOLY LAND
IN THE TIME OF CHRIST

LOCATIONS where principal events occurred in Part II

1. CAPERNAUM—Here disciples have argument about who will be the greatest in Jesus' Kingdom (See page 53)
2. JERUSALEM—Principal City of Palestine (See pages 55, 58-61, 65, 68, 69, 71, 73, 76, 87, 94, 97)
3. SAMARIA—A district in Palestine. Also a city by that name (See pages 58, 61)
4. POOL OF SILOAM—Here a blind man was told to wash and received his sight (See page 59)
5. CHORAZIN and BETHSAIDA—Two cities where Jesus was not received hospitably (See page 60)
6. JERICHO—A city on the road leading from Jerusalem where the Good Samaritan befriended a man (See page 61)
7. BETHANY—The home of Martha and Mary (See pages 62, 68, 72, 73, 97)
8. PEREA—The country east of the Jordan where many came to meet Jesus (See pages 58, 65)
9. JORDAN RIVER—Principal river in Palestine (See page 65)
10. MOUNT OF OLIVES (Olivet)—Noted mountain of hills east of Jerusalem where Jesus talks with His disciples (See page 77)
11. GARDEN OF GETHSEMANE—Here Jesus was betrayed and arrested (See page 83)
12. GALILEE—Northern district of Palestine (See pages 86, 87, 91, 93, 96)
13. SEA OF GALILEE—Scene of a great catch of fish (See page 95)
14. GOLGOTHA (Calvary)—A hill near Jerusalem where Jesus was crucified (See page 90)
15. ARIMATHEA—Home of Joseph in whose tomb the body of Jesus was placed (See page 92)
16. EMMAUS—Home of two followers of Jesus with whom Jesus talked after His resurrection (See page 94)

PHOENICIA
GALILEE
CHORAZIN
CAPERNAUM
BETHSAIDA
Sea of Galilee
Hippos R.
SAMARIA
SAMARIA
Jordan River
Jabbok R.
ARIMATHEA
PEREA
EMMAUS
JERICHO
JERUSALEM
JUDEA
Dead Sea
Arnon R.

N
W E
S

Scale of Miles
0   10   20   30   40   50

ROMAN ROAD
ROMAN ROAD
MODERN ROAD
(CALVARY) GOLGOTHA
JERUSALEM
GETHSEMANE
Mt. of Olives
Bethphage
Bethany
POOL OF SILOAM
PLAIN OF REPHAIM

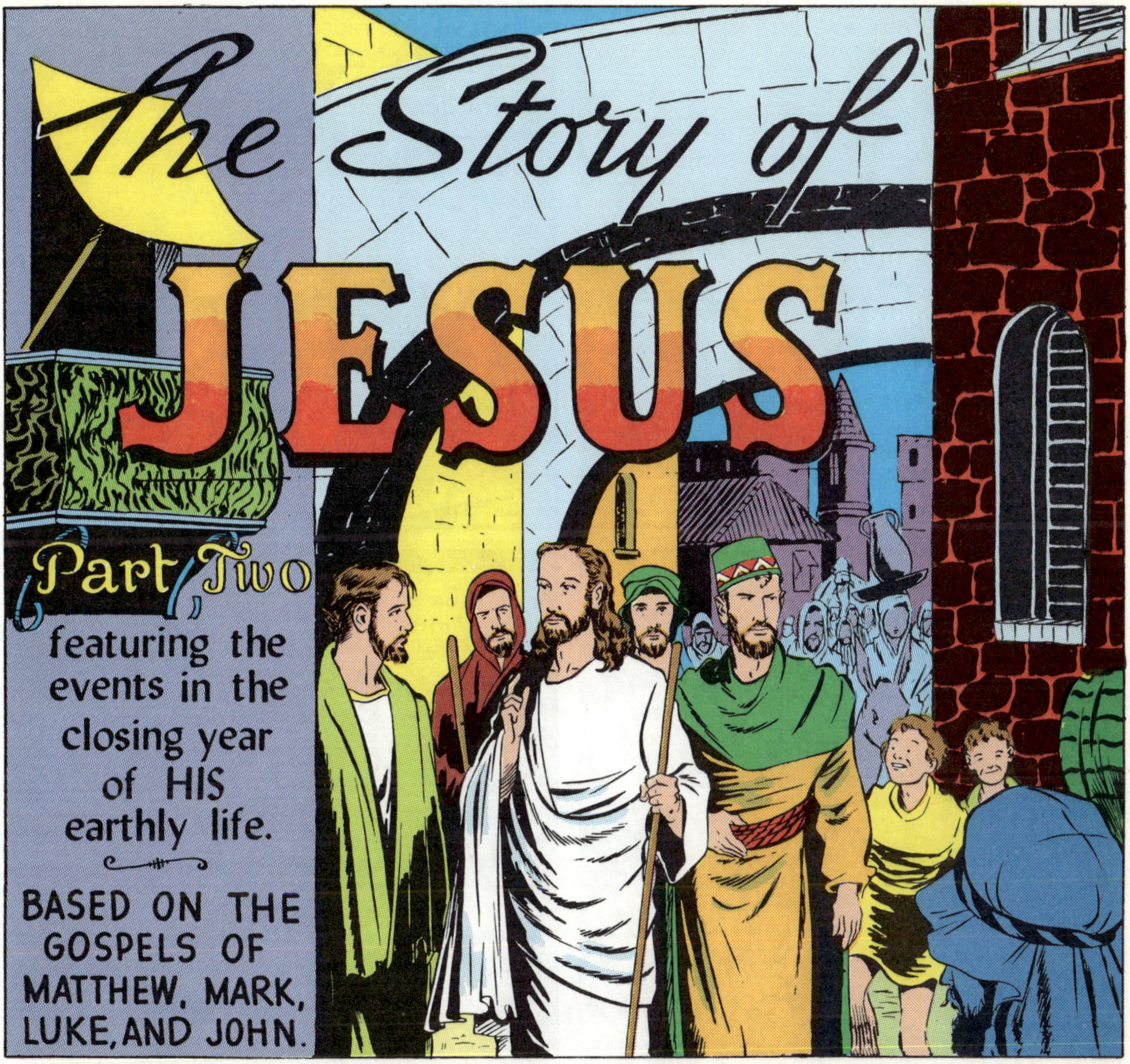

The Story of JESUS

Part Two

featuring the events in the closing year of HIS earthly life.

BASED ON THE GOSPELS OF MATTHEW, MARK, LUKE, AND JOHN.

Matthew 18:1-3, Mark 9:33-36, Luke 9:46-48

Matthew 18:4-6, 18:21-28

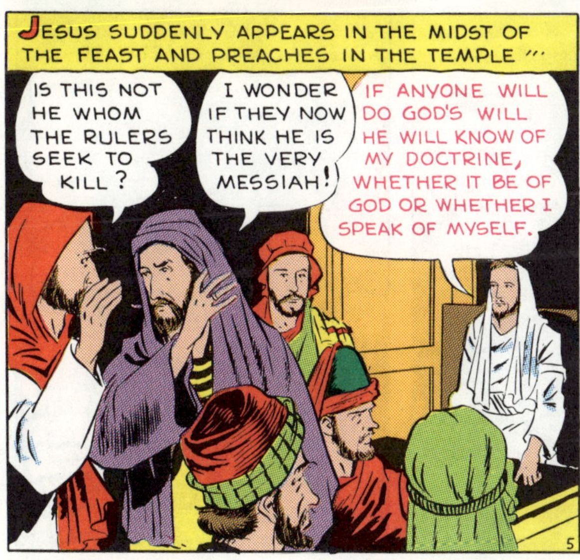

Matthew 18:29-35, Matthew 13:55, John 7:1-52

EARLY IN THE TEMPLE, ONE MORNING, CERTAIN SCRIBES AND PHARISEES BRING A WOMAN TO JESUS ―――
MASTER, THIS WOMAN HAS SINNED!
MOSES, IN HIS LAW, SAYS SHE SHOULD BE STONED—WHAT DO YOU SAY?
THEY ARE TRYING TO TRICK JESUS INTO SAYING SOMETHING TO ACCUSE HIM!
HE THAT IS WITHOUT SIN AMONG YOU, LET HIM FIRST CAST A STONE AT HER!

THE WOMAN'S ACCUSERS WITH GUILTY CONSCIENCES SLINK AWAY—
WOMAN WHERE ARE THOSE THINE ACCUSERS? HATH NO MAN CONDEMNED THEE? NEITHER DO I. —GO, AND SIN NO MORE.

JESUS TEACHES IN THE TREASURY OF THE TEMPLE
I AM THE LIGHT OF THE WORLD— HE THAT FOLLOWETH ME SHALL NOT WALK IN DARKNESS, BUT, HAVE THE LIGHT OF LIFE!
YOU BEAR WITNESS OF YOURSELF— HOW DO YOU EXPECT US TO BELIEVE YOU?

IT IS WRITTEN IN THE LAW, THAT THE TESTIMONY OF TWO MEN IS TRUE— I BEAR WITNESS OF MYSELF AND THE FATHER WHO SENT ME, BEARETH WITNESS!
WHERE IS YOUR FATHER?

YE NEITHER KNOW ME NOR MY FATHER—IF YE HAD KNOWN ME, YE WOULD HAVE KNOWN MY FATHER ALSO—I GO MY WAY—WHITHER I GO YE CANNOT COME!
WILL HE KILL HIMSELF?
THIS IS STRANGE TALK I CAN'T UNDERSTAND!

JESUS SPEAKS OF HIS COMING CRUCIFIXION, BUT, HE IS NOT UNDERSTOOD THEN ―――
WHEN YE HAVE LIFTED UP THE SON OF MAN, THEN SHALL YE KNOW THAT I AM HE, EVEN THE SAME THAT I SAID FROM THE BEGINNING!
I DON'T KNOW WHAT HE MEANS BY BEING LIFTED UP!
HE SPEAKS WITH SINCERITY —I BELIEVE IN HIM!

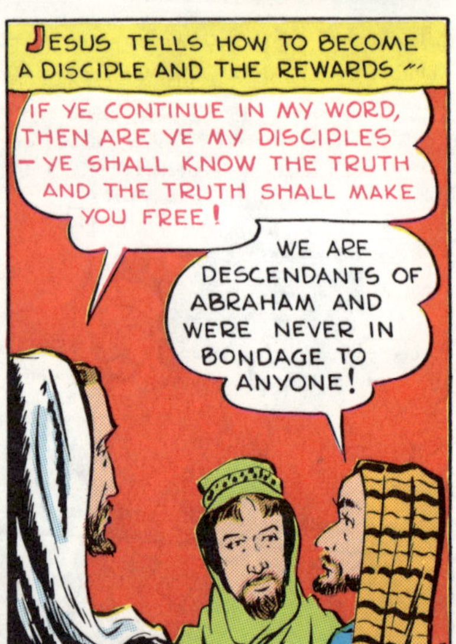
JESUS TELLS HOW TO BECOME A DISCIPLE AND THE REWARDS ―――
IF YE CONTINUE IN MY WORD, THEN ARE YE MY DISCIPLES —YE SHALL KNOW THE TRUTH AND THE TRUTH SHALL MAKE YOU FREE!
WE ARE DESCENDANTS OF ABRAHAM AND WERE NEVER IN BONDAGE TO ANYONE!

John 8:1-33

WHOSOEVER COMMITTETH SIN IS THE SERVANT OF SIN — IF YE WERE ABRAHAM'S CHILDREN YE WOULD DO THE WORKS OF ABRAHAM — NOW YE SEEK TO KILL ONE WHO HATH TOLD YOU THE TRUTH!

THE RELIGIOUS LEADERS CONTINUE TO DISPUTE WITH JESUS
WE HAVE ONE FATHER, EVEN GOD!
IF GOD WERE YOUR FATHER YE WOULD LOVE ME, FOR I AM FROM GOD — YE ARE OF YOUR FATHER THE DEVIL …A MURDERER… AND A LIAR!

IT IS YOU WHO HAVE A DEVIL!
HE THAT IS OF GOD HEARETH GOD'S WORDS. — YE … HEAR THEM NOT BECAUSE YE ARE NOT OF GOD!

JESUS MAKES AN ASTOUNDING STATEMENT!
IF ANY MAN KEEPS MY SAYINGS, HE SHALL NEVER SEE DEATH!
NOW, WE KNOW YOU HAVE A DEVIL!
ARE YOU GREATER THAN OUR FATHER ABRAHAM WHO IS DEAD?

IT IS MY FATHER WHO HONORETH ME — YE SAY HE IS YOUR GOD — YET YE HAVE NOT KNOWN HIM — ABRAHAM REJOICED TO SEE MY DAY AND WAS GLAD!
YOU ARE NOT YET FIFTY YEARS OLD, AND DO YOU MEAN TO SAY YOU SAW ABRAHAM?

JESUS' ADMISSION THAT HE LIVED BEFORE ABRAHAM AROUSES ANGER
VERILY, I SAY UNTO YOU. I WAS BEFORE ABRAHAM!
HE DESERVES TO BE STONED FOR SUCH STATEMENTS!

BUT JESUS HID HIMSELF FROM THE CROWD, AND ESCAPED UNHARMED.

John 8:34-59

Mark 10:1, Luke 9:51-62

JESUS' DISCIPLES IN JERUSALEM QUESTION HIM ABOUT A BLIND BEGGAR '''
MASTER, WHO SINNED, THIS MAN OR HIS PARENTS THAT HE WAS BORN BLIND?
NEITHER HATH THIS MAN SINNED, NOR HIS PARENTS, BUT THAT THE WORKS OF GOD SHOULD BE MADE MANIFEST IN HIM!

JESUS MAKES CLAY AND PLACES IT ON THE MAN'S EYES
GO WASH IN THE POOL OF SILOAM!

WHEN THE MAN WASHES, AS DIRECTED, HIS SIGHT IS RESTORED '''
PRAISE GOD, I CAN SEE!

CROWDS GATHER TO DISCUSS HIS CURE — — SOME OF THE PHARISEES TRY TO CONFUSE HIM
YES, IT IS HE THAT SAT AND BEGGED!
WHO CURED YOU?
A MAN WHO IS CALLED JESUS. WHO OR WHERE HE IS, I KNOW NOT!
I WON'T BELIEVE HE WAS BLIND UNTIL HIS PARENTS TELL US!

THE PHARISEES QUESTION THE MAN'S PARENTS WHO ARE AFRAID THAT CREDITING THE CURE TO JESUS, WILL PUT THEM OUT OF THE SYNAGOGUE.
IS THIS YOUR SON WHO WAS BLIND? —HOW THEN DOES HE NOW SEE?
YES, HE IS OUR SON WHO WAS BLIND FROM BIRTH. WHO OPENED HIS EYES WE KNOW NOT— HE'S OF AGE, ASK HIM!

SO THE ANGRY PHARISEES QUESTION THE MAN AGAIN AND SAY JESUS IS A SINNER BECAUSE HE CURED ON THE SABBATH '''
WHETHER HE IS A SINNER OR NOT, I KNOW NOT, BUT ONE THING I KNOW, WHEREAS I WAS BLIND, NOW I SEE!
YOU WERE BORN IN SIN — DO YOU WANT TO TEACH US? GET OUT OF THE SYNAGOGUE!

WHEN JESUS LEARNS THAT HE WAS CAST OUT, HE COMES TO HIM.
DOST THOU BELIEVE ON THE SON OF GOD WHO TALKETH TO THEE?
IF YOU ARE HE, LORD, I BELIEVE!

John 9:1-38

Matthew 11:25-30, Luke 10:1-24

A LAWYER ASKS JESUS HOW TO OBTAIN ETERNAL LIFE, HE IS TOLD TO LOVE HIS GOD AND HIS NEIGHBOR ...
I AGREE I SHOULD LOVE MY NEIGHBOR, BUT WHO IS MY NEIGHBOR?
A CERTAIN MAN WENT DOWN FROM JERUSALEM TO JERICHO
JESUS TELLS A PARABLE

HE FELL AMONG THIEVES WHO STRIPPED HIM OF HIS RAIMENT
QUICK - HAND OVER YOUR MONEY!
YOU COWARDS - NOT ONE OF YOU, ALONE, COULD DO THIS!

THEY WOUNDED HIM ... LEAVING HIM HALF DEAD
SERVES HIM RIGHT TO PUT UP SUCH A FIGHT!
VERY LITTLE MONEY TOO, FOR US THREE!

BY CHANCE, THERE CAME DOWN A CERTAIN PRIEST WHO LOOKED ON HIM AND PASSED BY ...
I'D LIKE TO HELP HIM BUT I'M LATE FOR THE SERVICES NOW!

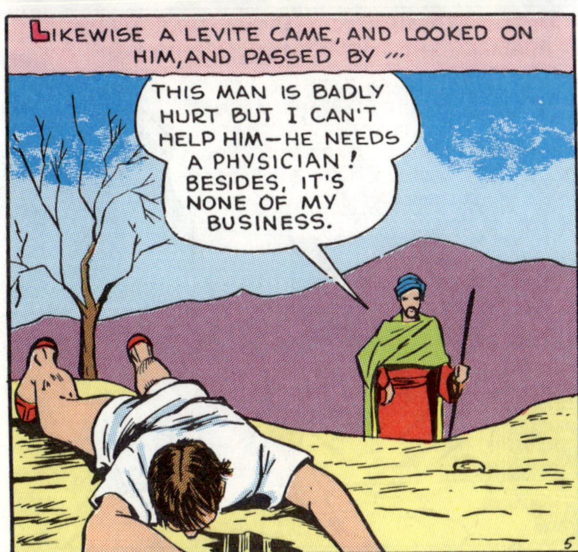
LIKEWISE A LEVITE CAME, AND LOOKED ON HIM, AND PASSED BY ...
THIS MAN IS BADLY HURT BUT I CAN'T HELP HIM—HE NEEDS A PHYSICIAN! BESIDES, IT'S NONE OF MY BUSINESS.

BUT A SAMARITAN, WHOSE PEOPLE WERE SCORNED, HAD COMPASSION --- BOUND UP HIS WOUNDS AND BROUGHT HIM TO AN INN ...
NOW WITH YOUR WOUNDS WASHED OUT WITH MY OIL AND WINE, WE'LL GO TO THE INN!

AND IN THE MORNING HE DEPARTED
TAKE GOOD CARE OF HIM, INN-KEEPER — IF IT COSTS MORE I'LL PAY YOU ON MY NEXT TRIP!

WHICH OF THESE THREE WAS A NEIGHBOR?
HE WHO SHOWED PITY AND YOU SAY I SHOULD DO LIKEWISE!

IN BETHANY LIVED TWO SISTERS, MARTHA AND MARY
PLEASE, LORD, COME AND DINE WITH MARY AND ME!

MARY LISTENS FASCINATED AT JESUS' WORDS
MARY, YOU SHOULD HELP ME! LORD, DON'T YOU THINK SHE'S NOT CONSIDERATE TO LET ME DO ALL THE WORK ALONE?

JESUS REBUKES MARTHA
MARTHA, MARTHA, THOU ART TROUBLED ABOUT MANY THINGS!
MARTHA, I FELT I MUST HEAR JESUS. HE SEEMS MORE INTERESTED IN TELLING US HOW TO LIVE, THAN IN EATING!
FORGIVE ME! BUT DINNER IS READY!

JESUS EXPLAINS TO MARTHA THAT MARY REALIZES THE IMPORTANCE OF HIS WORDS.
BUT ONE THING IS NEEDED AND MARY HATH CHOSEN THAT GOOD PART WHICH SHALL NOT BE TAKEN AWAY FROM HER!

Luke 10:35-42

As JESUS FINISHES PRAYING ONE DAY, A DISCIPLE ASKS HOW TO PRAY
LORD, TEACH US TO PRAY EVEN AS JOHN THE BAPTIST ALSO TAUGHT HIS DISCIPLES!
PRAYER MUST BE IMPORTANT— YOU PRAY CONSTANTLY!

JESUS GIVES THEM A MODEL PRAYER (CALLED THE LORD'S PRAYER) ···
OUR FATHER WHO ART IN HEAVEN, HALLOWED BE THY NAME, THY KINGDOM COME, THY WILL BE DONE, IN EARTH AS IT IS DONE IN HEAVEN—GIVE US THIS DAY OUR DAILY BREAD AND FORGIVE US OUR DEBTS AS WE FORGIVE OUR DEBTORS; AND LEAD US NOT INTO TEMPTATION BUT DELIVER US FROM EVIL, FOR THINE IS THE KINGDOM AND THE POWER AND THE GLORY FOREVER — AMEN

BY A QUESTION—PARABLE JESUS CONTINUES ···
WHICH OF YOU SHALL HAVE A FRIEND AND GO UNTO HIM AT MIDNIGHT!
IT'S LATE BUT LEND ME THREE LOAVES OF BREAD A FRIEND HAS JUST COME FROM A LONG JOURNEY!
DON'T BOTHER ME — I CAN'T GIVE YOU BREAD AT THIS TIME— IT'S TOO LATE, BESIDES MY CHILDREN ARE IN BED!

"THOUGH HE WILL NOT RISE AND GIVE HIM BECAUSE HE IS HIS FRIEND, BUT BECAUSE OF HIS URGENT REQUEST, HE WILL ARISE AND GIVE HIM BREAD ···
YOU CERTAINLY ARE PERSISTENT — WILL THREE LOAVES BE ENOUGH?
THANKS THEY'LL HELP ME A LOT!

JESUS GIVES THREE SUGGESTIONS FOR PRAYING ···
ASK AND IT SHALL BE GIVEN YOU
SEEK AND YE SHALL FIND
KNOCK AND IT SHALL BE OPENED UNTO YOU —

ANOTHER PARABLE PICTURES GOD AS A GENEROUS FATHER ···
FATHER, GIVE ME SOMETHING TO EAT —— SOME BREAD, FISH AND AN EGG!
SURELY, SON, YOU ARE HUNGRY AND I'D BE CRUEL TO OFFER YOU THESE STONES SHAPED LIKE BREAD, OR THIS SERPENT RESEMBLING A FISH OR THIS WHITE AND ROUND SCORPION LOOKING LIKE AN EGG!

IF YE THEN, BEING EVIL, KNOW HOW TO GIVE GOOD GIFTS UNTO YOUR CHILDREN — HOW MUCH MORE SHALL YOUR HEAVENLY FATHER GIVE THE HOLY SPIRIT TO THEM THAT ASK HIM?

JESUS' MIRACLES AND SAYINGS CONTINUE TO AMAZE THE PEOPLE ---
WHY DO YOU BREAK OUR TRADITIONS AND NOT WASH BEFORE EATING?
YE PHARISEES CLEANSE THE OUTSIDE --- BUT YOUR INWARD PART IS FULL OF EXTORTION AND WICKEDNESS!

JESUS, KNOWING THE MOTIVES OF SOME PHARISEES, TO TRAP HIM, SPEAKS OUT.
WOE UNTO YOU PHARISEES! YE GIVE A TENTH --- BUT PASS OVER JUSTICE AND THE LOVE OF GOD --- YE LOVE THE CHIEF SEATS IN THE SYNAGOGUES AND SALUTATIONS IN THE MARKET PLACES --- YE ARE TOMBS OVER WHICH MEN WALK!

JESUS ALSO REBUKES THE LAWYER-GUEST ---
TEACHER, THAT'S STRONG LANGUAGE. IT REPROACHES US LAWYERS ALSO!
WOE UNTO YOU, LAWYERS TOO --- YE LOAD MEN WITH BURDENS YET TOUCH THEM NOT WITH ONE OF YOUR FINGERS --- YOUR FATHERS KILLED THE PROPHETS AND YE BUILD THEM TOMBS!

JESUS TELLS THE LAWYER THAT GOD SENT PROPHETS AND APOSTLES WHOM THE PEOPLE KILLED, AFRAID TO HEAR UNPLEASANT TRUTHS ---
WOE UNTO YOU --- YE TOOK AWAY THE KEYS OF KNOWLEDGE --- AND ENTER NOT IN YOURSELVES, BUT HINDER THEM WHO WOULD ENTER!

"AND WHEN HE WAS COME OUT FROM THENCE, THE SCRIBES AND THE PHARISEES BEGAN TO PRESS UPON HIM VEHEMENTLY, AND TO PROVOKE HIM TO SPEAK OF MANY THINGS, LAYING WAIT FOR HIM, TO CATCH SOMETHING OUT OF HIS MOUTH ---
LUKE 11: 53-54

IN JERUSALEM, ONE WINTER DAY, DURING THE JEWISH FEAST OF THE DEDICATION, A CROWD GATHERS ABOUT JESUS
HOW LONG WILL YOU KEEP US IN SUSPENSE?
YES, TELL US IF YOU ARE THE MESSIAH!
I TOLD YOU AND YE BELIEVE NOT—THE WORKS THAT I DO IN MY FATHER'S NAME·· BEAR WITNESS OF ME!

DO YOU KNOW WHY WE DON'T BELIEVE IN YOU?
BECAUSE YE ARE NOT OF MY SHEEP—MY SHEEP HEAR MY VOICE··· I KNOW THEM AND THEY FOLLOW ME—I GIVE UNTO THEM ETERNAL LIFE—NO ONE IS ABLE TO SNATCH THEM OUT OF MY FATHER'S HAND—I AND MY FATHER ARE ONE!

ANGERED AT JESUS' CLAIMS, SOME ARE READY TO STONE HIM
HE IS A BLASPHEMER! HE DESERVES TO BE STONED!
YES, HE CLAIMS TO BE THE SON OF GOD!
MANY GOOD WORKS I HAVE SHOWED YOU FROM THE FATHER, FOR WHICH WOULD YOU STONE ME? BELIEVE THE WORKS, THAT YOU MAY KNOW THAT THE FATHER IS IN ME AND I IN THE FATHER!

THEY SOUGHT AGAIN TO TAKE HIM BUT HE ESCAPED OUT OF THEIR HANDS
WHY DOESN'T SOMEONE STONE HIM?
NO ONE IS WILLING TO THROW THE FIRST STONE!

JESUS NOW AGAIN GOES INTO PEREA, ACROSS THE RIVER JORDAN
THERE'S THE JORDAN! ACROSS IT, IS WHERE JOHN THE BAPTIST FIRST TOLD US ABOUT YOU!
THROUGH JOHN WE BECAME YOUR DISCIPLES—HE DID NO MIRACLES!

AND ACROSS THE JORDAN, JESUS ABODE AND MANY FLOCKED TO HIM
IS THAT JESUS ABOUT WHOM YOU TOLD US?
YES, CHILD, WE FIRST LEARNED ABOUT HIM LISTENING TO JOHN THE BAPTIST!
YES, WE CAME TO BELIEVE IN JESUS AND TO LOVE HIM LIKE YOU AND YOUR BROTHER WILL TOO!

John 10:22-42

JESUS, ONE SABBATH, EATS WITH PHARISEES AND LAWYERS — HE IS WATCHED SUSPICIOUSLY AS A MAN WITH DROPSY PLEADS
MASTER, I IMPLORE YOU TO HEAL ME!
IS IT LAWFUL TO HEAL ON THE SABBATH?

JESUS HEALS THE MAN AMIDST THE SILENT DISAPPROVAL OF ALL
THANK YOU, LORD, I AM CURED!
WHICH OF YOU SHALL HAVE AN ASS OR AN OX FALLEN INTO A PIT AND WILL NOT STRAIGHTWAY DRAW HIM OUT ON THE SABBATH DAY?

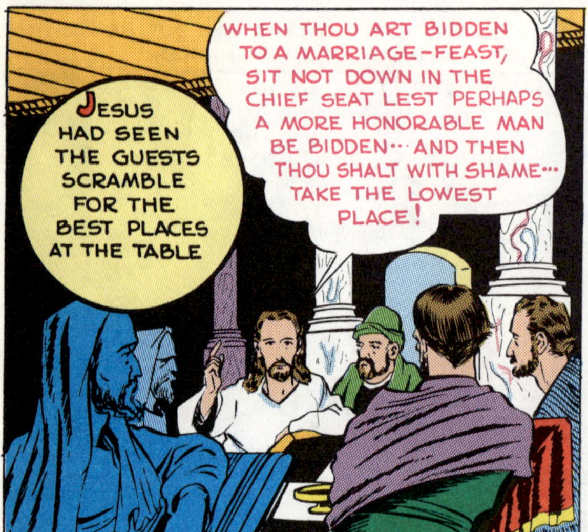
JESUS HAD SEEN THE GUESTS SCRAMBLE FOR THE BEST PLACES AT THE TABLE
WHEN THOU ART BIDDEN TO A MARRIAGE-FEAST, SIT NOT DOWN IN THE CHIEF SEAT LEST PERHAPS A MORE HONORABLE MAN BE BIDDEN… AND THEN THOU SHALT WITH SHAME… TAKE THE LOWEST PLACE!

BUT WHEN BIDDEN, GO AND SIT DOWN IN THE LOWEST PLACE, THAT WHEN HE THAT HATH BIDDEN SAY… FRIEND GO UP HIGHER… THEN THOU SHALT HAVE GLORY IN THE PRESENCE OF ALL!

EVERY ONE WHO EXALTETH HIMSELF SHALL BE HUMBLED BUT HE THAT HUMBLETH HIMSELF SHALL BE EXHALTED!

JESUS SPEAKS TO THOSE WHO HAD INVITED HIM
WHEN THOU MAKEST A DINNER OR A SUPPER, CALL NOT THY FRIENDS, NOR THY BRETHREN, NEITHER THY KINSMEN, NOR THY RICH NEIGHBORS — LEST THEY ALSO BID THEE AGAIN, AND A RECOMPENSE BE MADE THEE — BUT WHEN THOU MAKEST A FEAST, CALL THE POOR, THE MAIMED, THE LAME, THE BLIND — AND THOU SHALT BE BLESSED — FOR THEY CANNOT RECOMPENSE THEE — FOR THOU SHALT BE RECOMPENSED AT THE RESURRECTION OF THE JUST!

SOME OF THE RELIGIOUS LEADERS OBJECTED TO JESUS ASSOCIATING WITH ALL CLASSES OF PEOPLE
THIS MAN RECEIVETH SINNERS AND EATETH WITH THEM!
THE LOST SHEEP
WHAT MAN OF YOU, HAVING A HUNDRED SHEEP AND LOSING ONE, DOTH NOT···GO AFTER THAT··· AND WHEN HE HATH FOUND IT··· CALLETH TOGETHER HIS FRIENDS AND NEIGHBORS SAYING, REJOICE WITH ME!

LIKEWISE THERE IS JOY IN HEAVEN OVER ONE SINNER THAT REPENTETH MORE THAN OVER NINETY AND NINE JUST PERSONS WHO NEED NO REPENTANCE!

THE LOST COIN
WHAT WOMAN HAVING TEN PIECES OF SILVER AND LOSING ONE DOTH NOT LIGHT A CANDLE, SWEEP THE HOUSE AND SEEK DILIGENTLY TILL SHE FIND IT— THEN SHE CALLS HER NEIGHBORS AND FRIENDS SAYING, REJOICE WITH ME FOR I HAVE FOUND THE PIECE THAT WAS LOST— LIKEWISE THERE IS JOY IN THE PRESENCE OF ANGELS OF GOD OVER ONE SINNER THAT REPENTETH!

THE PRODIGAL SON
"A CERTAIN MAN HAD TWO SONS"
ALL RIGHT SON, HERE'S YOUR SHARE-VERY SORRY YOU ARE LEAVING!
FATHER GIVE ME THE SHARE OF WHAT'S COMING TO ME- I WANT TO GET AWAY AND LIVE MY OWN LIFE!

"THE YOUNGER SON TOOK HIS JOURNEY INTO A FAR COUNTRY AND WASTED HIS SUBSTANCE WITH RIOTOUS LIVING"
YOU'RE A GREAT SPORT!
MORE FUN, EH? THAN ON THE FARM WITH THE OLD MAN AND MY NAGGING BROTHER!
HAVE SOME MORE WINE!

"AND WHEN HE HAD SPENT ALL, THERE AROSE A MIGHTY FAMINE IN THAT LAND — AND HE BEGAN TO BE IN WANT"
ONLY JOB OPEN IS TAKING CARE OF MY PIGS!
I'VE GOT TO EAT — I'LL TAKE IT!
"AND WHEN HE CAME TO HIMSELF HE SAID, HOW MANY OF MY FATHER'S HIRED SERVANTS HAVE FOOD ENOUGH AND TO SPARE, AND I PERISH WITH HUNGER — I WILL ARISE AND GO TO MY FATHER"

"WHEN HE WAS A GREAT WAY OFF, HIS FATHER SAW HIM AND HAD COMPASSION ON HIM AND RAN AND FELL ON HIS NECK AND KISSED HIM"
FATHER I HAVE SINNED AGAINST HEAVEN AND IN THY SIGHT AND AM NO MORE WORTHY TO BE CALLED THY SON!
—"AND BRING HITHER THE FATTED CALF AND KILL IT —, FOR THIS, MY SON, WAS DEAD AND IS ALIVE AGAIN; HE WAS LOST AND IS FOUND."
FOR THE SON OF MAN CAME TO SEEK AND TO SAVE THAT WHICH WAS LOST ···
LUKE 19:10

MARY AND HER SISTER MARTHA WHO LIVE AT BETHANY SEND WORD TO JESUS, IN JERUSALEM, TO COME AND CURE THEIR BROTHER LAZARUS, WHO IS SERIOUSLY SICK
YOU MUST NOT GO TO BETHANY, PEOPLE THERE ARE READY TO STONE YOU!
LAZARUS IS DEAD.. NEVERTHELESS LET US GO UNTO HIM ――
LET US GO WITH JESUS EVEN IF WE MUST DIE WITH HIM!

MARTHA, GRIEVING FOR HER DEAD BROTHER, RUNS AHEAD.. TO GREET JESUS
LORD, IF YOU HAD BEEN HERE MY BROTHER WOULD NOT HAVE DIED —BUT EVEN NOW WHATEVER YOU ASK OF GOD HE WILL DO IT!
THY BROTHER SHALL RISE AGAIN···I AM THE RESURRECTION AND THE LIFE—HE THAT BELIEVETH IN ME, THOUGH HE WERE DEAD, YET SHALL HE LIVE!

MARY TOO, COMES OUT TO MEET JESUS
OH MASTER, IF ONLY YOU HAD BEEN HERE!
SEE JESUS IS WEEPING!
COULD NOT HE WHO DID THE OTHER MIRACLES HAVE KEPT LAZARUS FROM DYING?
WHERE HAVE YOU LAID HIM?

JESUS COMES TO THE TOMB WHERE LAZARUS' BODY HAS BEEN PLACED
MARTHA, SAID I NOT UNTO THEE THAT IF THOU WOULDST BELIEVE THOU SHOULDST SEE THE GLORY OF GOD?

JESUS PRAYS BEFORE THE OPEN TOMB
FATHER, I THANK THEE THAT THOU HAST HEARD ME ···

MARTHA AND MARY WITH THEIR FRIENDS LOOK ON WITH AMAZEMENT AS LAZARUS IS SEEN RISING FROM THE DEAD
LAZARUS COME FORTH!
OH BROTHER, THROUGH JESUS YOU ARE MADE ALIVE!
MOST AMAZING! A MAN DEAD AND NOW ALIVE!
THEN MANY·· WHO CAME·· AND HAD SEEN THE THINGS THAT JESUS DID BELIEVED IN HIM

John 11:1-45

AS JESUS JOURNEYS TO JERUSALEM FOR THE LAST TIME, TEN MEN WITH LEPROSY CALL TO HIM '''
JESUS, MASTER, HAVE MERCY ON US!
IF YOU WILL YOU CAN CURE US!
GO - SHOW YOURSELVES UNTO THE PRIESTS!

AS JESUS SPEAKS THE MEN FEEL THAT THEY ARE CURED AND START TO GO TO THE PRIESTS WHO ONLY HAVE AUTHORITY TO PRONOUNCE THEM CURED '''
LOOK SEE I'M CURED!
YES, ME TOO - NOW I'M LIKE OTHER MEN!
I'M GOING BACK TO THANK JESUS!

ONE OF THE TEN WITH LEPROSY RETURNS TO JESUS
WERE THERE NOT TEN CLEANSED? BUT WHERE ARE THE NINE? ARISE, GO THY WAY, THY FAITH HATH MADE THEE WHOLE!
I AM A SAMARITAN CURED OF MY LEPROSY THANKS TO YOU!

JESUS TELLS A PARABLE REBUKING SELF-RIGHTEOUS PEOPLE WHO FEEL THEY ARE BETTER THAN OTHERS '''
TWO MEN WENT UP INTO THE TEMPLE TO PRAY - THE ONE A PHARISEE AND THE OTHER A PUBLIGAN!

I THANK GOD THAT I AM NOT LIKE OTHER MEN, OR EVEN THIS PUBLICAN - I FAST... AND GIVE TITHES!
GOD BE MERCIFUL TO ME A SINNER!

I TELL YOU THAT THIS PUBLICAN WENT DOWN TO HIS HOUSE JUSTIFIED RATHER THAN THE OTHER — FOR EVERYONE WHO EXALTETH HIMSELF SHALL BE ABASED AND HE THAT HUMBLETH HIMSELF SHALL BE EXALTED!

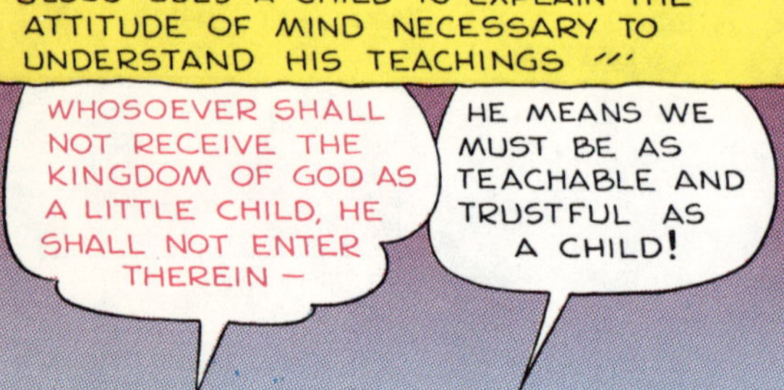

Matthew 19:13-30, Mark 10:13-31, Luke 18:15-30

Matthew 20:17-29, Mark 10:32-45, Luke 18:31-34, 19:1-10

Matthew 26:6-13, Mark 14:3-9, John 12:1-11

Matthew 21:1-27, Mark 11:1-33, Luke 19:29-40, John 12:12-19

Matthew 21:33-41

SOME PHARISEES CONSPIRED WITH THE HERODIANS, A GROUP CLOSE TO THE AUTHORITIES, TO REPORT ANY UNPATRIOTIC UTTERANCE OF JESUS, SO HE MIGHT BE ARRESTED
MASTER, WE KNOW YOU TEACH THE WAYS OF GOD AND ARE NOT AFRAID TO TELL THE TRUTH — IS IT RIGHT FOR US JEWS TO PAY TAXES TO THE ROMANS?
YE HYPOCRITES! THIS TRIBUTE MONEY! WHOSE IS THIS IMAGE AND SUPER-SCRIPTION?
THAT IS CAESAR!

RENDER THEREFORE UNTO CAESAR, THE THINGS THAT ARE CAESAR'S, AND UNTO GOD THE THINGS THAT ARE GOD'S!
THAT CATCH QUESTION DID NOT FOOL JESUS!
IT'S MARVELOUS HOW HE ANSWERS THEM!

NOW THE SADDUCEES, A RELIGIOUS SECT WHO DID NOT BELIEVE IN A HEREAFTER, TRY TO TRAP JESUS
MASTER, MOSES SAID IF A MAN DIED HAVING NO CHILDREN, HIS BROTHER IS EXPECTED TO MARRY HIS WIFE AND RAISE UP CHILDREN — NOW THERE WERE SEVEN BROTHERS — THE FIRST DIED, AND THE SECOND BROTHER MARRIED HIS WIFE — ALSO THE THIRD MARRIED THE WIFE SO ON UP TO THE SEVENTH BROTHER — AT LAST THE WOMAN DIED — IN THE RESURRECTION WHOSE WIFE SHALL SHE BE?
YE DO ERR NOT KNOWING THE SCRIPTURES — IN THE RESURRECTION THEY NEITHER MARRY NOR ARE GIVEN IN MAR-RIAGE, BUT ARE AS THE ANGELS OF GOD IN HEAVEN!
HE SHOWED UP THE SADDUCEES TOO!

THE PHARISEES TRY AGAIN TO CONFUSE JESUS THROUGH ONE OF THEIR NUMBER, WHO IS A LAWYER
MASTER, WHICH IS THE GREAT COMMANDMENT IN THE LAW?
THOU SHALT LOVE THE LORD THY GOD WITH ALL THY HEART AND SOUL AND MIND — THIS IS THE FIRST AND GREAT COMMANDMENT, — THE SECOND IS LIKE UNTO IT, THOU SHALT LOVE THY NEIGHBOR AS THYSELF — ON THESE TWO COMMANDMENTS HANG ALL LAW AND THE PROPHETS!

MASTER, YOU HAVE TOLD THE TRUTH! — THERE IS ONE GOD, WHOM WE SHOULD LOVE WITH ALL OUR HEART AND UNDERSTANDING AND OUR SOUL — BUT TO LOVE OUR NEIGHBOR AS OURSELF IS MORE IMPORTANT THAN ANY BURNT OFFERINGS OR SACRIFICES!
JESUS SEES THE EARNESTNESS OF THE MAN
THOU ARE NOT FAR FROM THE KINGDOM OF GOD!
NO MAN AFTER THIS ASKS JESUS QUES-TIONS TO CATCH HIM

JESUS SPEAKS TO THE MULTITUDE AND DISCIPLES, WARNING THEM AGAINST THE TEACHING OF THE SCRIBES AND PHARISEES
THE SCRIBES AND PHARISEES LOVE TO BE SEEN OF MEN TO TAKE THE FIRST PLACES AT SUPPER AND FIRST SEATS AT THE SYNOGOGUES AND TO BE CALLED RABBI!

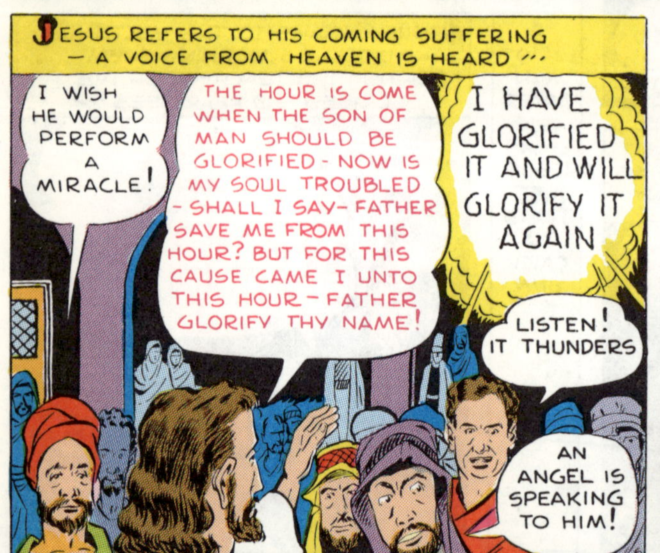

Matthew 23:13-37, Mark 12:41-44 Luke 21:1-4

Matthew 24:1-36, Mark 13:1-37, Luke 21:5-36

Matthew 25:1-13

Matthew 25:14-46

Matthew 26:1-5, 14:26, Mark 14:1-3, Luke 22:1-6, John 13:1-17

JESUS TELLS HIS DISCIPLES THAT ONE OF THEM WILL BETRAY HIM!
OUR MASTER LOOKS TROUBLED!
VERILY, VERILY, I SAY UNTO YOU, THAT ONE OF YOU SHALL BETRAY ME!

THE DISCIPLES INQUIRE WHO HE IS—PETER TELLS JOHN TO ASK JESUS ///
JESUS TELLS ME IT IS HE TO WHOM HE WILL HAND THE FOOD FROM THE EATING BOWL!
IS IT I?
MASTER, IS IT I?
WHAT THOU DOEST, DO QUICKLY!

JUDAS LEAVES TO COMPLETE THE BETRAYAL OF JESUS, WHILE JESUS SPEAKS EARNESTLY ///
A NEW COMMANDMENT I GIVE UNTO YOU—THAT YE LOVE ONE ANOTHER AS I HAVE LOVED YOU—BY THIS SHALL MEN KNOW THAT YE ARE MY DISCIPLES, IF YE HAVE LOVE ONE TO ANOTHER!
LORD, TO LOVE YOU IS NOT DIFFICULT, BUT WE DO NOT ALWAYS LOVE ONE ANOTHER!
BUT WE CAN REALLY SHOW OUR LOVE TO HIM BY LOVING EACH OTHER!

IN THIS FAREWELL CONVERSATION, JESUS GIVES WORDS OF COMFORT AND INSTRUCTION THAT ARE AMONG THE BEST REMEMBERED OF HIS WORDS TODAY ///
LET NOT YOUR HEART BE TROUBLED—I GO TO PREPARE A PLACE FOR YOU——AND WHITHER I GO YE KNOW THE WAY!
THOMAS, TELL HIM TO MAKE HIMSELF CLEAR!
LORD, WE DO NOT KNOW WHERE YOU ARE GOING NOR THE WAY!

I AM THE WAY—THE TRUTH AND THE LIFE; NO MAN COMETH UNTO THE FATHER BUT BY ME—HE WHO HATH SEEN ME HATH SEEN THE FATHER!
WE FIND IT DIFFICULT TO UNDERSTAND GOD WHO IS SPIRIT, BUT YOU, WE KNOW, ARE GOD MANIFESTED IN THE FLESH!

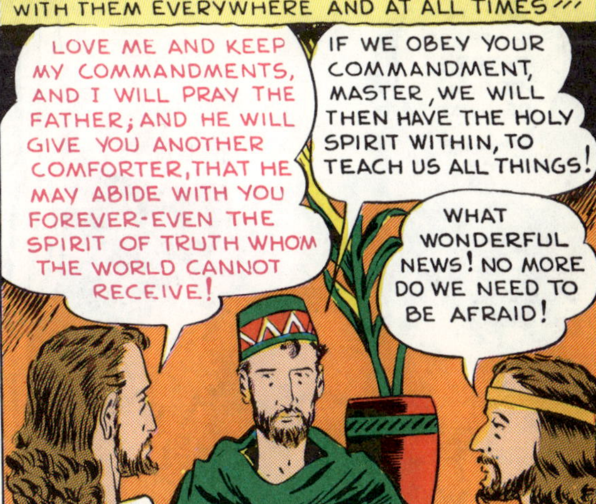
ALTHOUGH JESUS SAYS HE IS LEAVING THEM, HE PROMISES TO SEND HIS HOLY SPIRIT TO BE WITH THEM EVERYWHERE AND AT ALL TIMES ///
LOVE ME AND KEEP MY COMMANDMENTS, AND I WILL PRAY THE FATHER; AND HE WILL GIVE YOU ANOTHER COMFORTER, THAT HE MAY ABIDE WITH YOU FOREVER—EVEN THE SPIRIT OF TRUTH WHOM THE WORLD CANNOT RECEIVE!
IF WE OBEY YOUR COMMANDMENT, MASTER, WE WILL THEN HAVE THE HOLY SPIRIT WITHIN, TO TEACH US ALL THINGS!
WHAT WONDERFUL NEWS! NO MORE DO WE NEED TO BE AFRAID!

John 15:1-27, John 16:32-33

JESUS HAS A FAREWELL PRAYER WITH HIS DISCIPLES
THE HOUR HAS COME — GLORIFY THY SON···THOU HAST GIVEN HIM POWER OVER ALL FLESH THAT HE SHOULD GIVE ETERNAL LIFE··· AND THIS IS LIFE ETERNAL, THAT THEY MIGHT KNOW THEE···AND JESUS CHRIST WHOM THOU HAST SENT!

JESUS PRAYS FOR HIS DISCIPLES
I HAVE MANIFESTED THY NAME UNTO THESE MEN WHOM THOU GAVEST ME···THEY HAVE KEPT THY WORD··· AND HAVE KNOWN SURELY THAT I CAME FROM THEE AND THOU DIDST SEND ME. KEEP THOSE WHOM THOU HAST GIVEN ME, THAT THEY MAY BE ONE EVEN AS WE ARE··· THAT THEY MIGHT HAVE MY JOY FULFILLED IN THEMSELVES ···

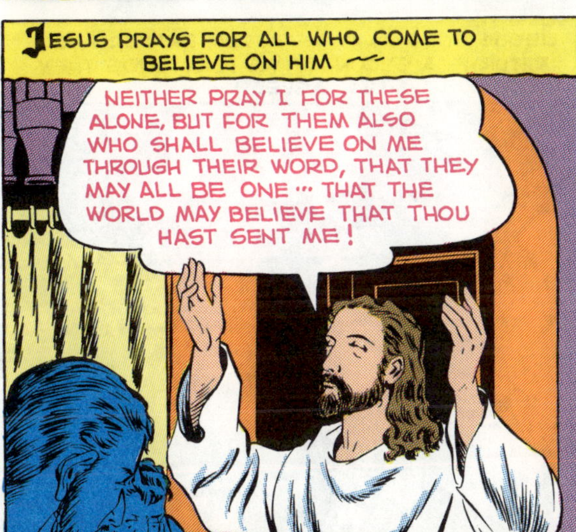
JESUS PRAYS FOR ALL WHO COME TO BELIEVE ON HIM ~
NEITHER PRAY I FOR THESE ALONE, BUT FOR THEM ALSO WHO SHALL BELIEVE ON ME THROUGH THEIR WORD, THAT THEY MAY ALL BE ONE ··· THAT THE WORLD MAY BELIEVE THAT THOU HAST SENT ME!

JESUS' PRAYER IS THAT OTHERS MAY COME TO KNOW AND FOLLOW HIS TEACHINGS ~~~
O RIGHTEOUS FATHER, THE WORLD HATH NOT KNOWN THEE — BUT I HAVE KNOWN THEE, AND THESE HAVE KNOWN THAT THOU HAST SENT ME··· AND THEY WILL DECLARE IT — THAT THE LOVE WHEREWITH THOU HAST LOVED ME MAY BE IN THEM AND I IN THEM!

BEFORE LEAVING THEY SING A HYMN

IN THE VERY EARLY MORNING OF FRIDAY, JESUS GOES WITH HIS DISCIPLES TO THE GARDEN OF GETHSEMANE ~~~
SIT YE HERE WHILE I GO AND PRAY YONDER!

Matthew 26:36-47, Mark 14:32-43, Luke 22:39-47, John 18:1-3

Matthew 26:48-68, Mark 14:44-65, Luke 22:48-53, John 18:4-14

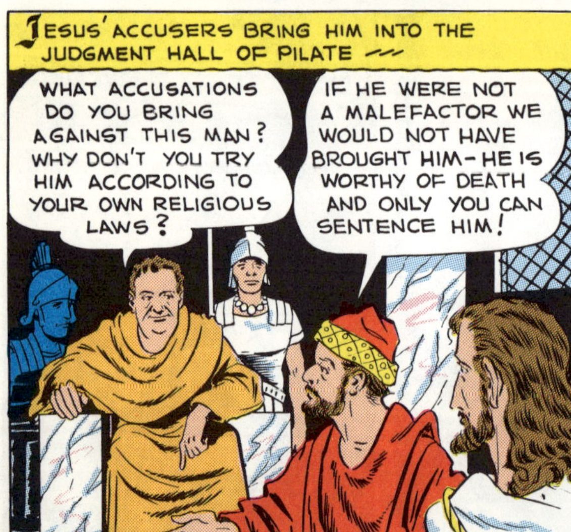

Matthew 26:69-75, Mark 14:66-72, 15:1-5, Luke 22:54-71, John 18:15-34

Matthew 27:1-2, Luke 23:1-16, John 18:35-38

AT THE TIME OF THE YEARLY FEAST OF THE PASSOVER IT IS CUSTOMARY TO RELEASE A PRISONER—PILATE BELIEVES THIS MAY BE AN OPPORTUNITY TO FREE JESUS ///
I HAVE WHIPPED JESUS—SHALL I LET HIM OR BARABBAS, WHO IS A ROBBER, AND MURDERER, GO FREE?
RELEASE BARABBAS!
CRUCIFY JESUS!

PILATE SEES THE MOB IS DETERMINED THAT JESUS BE KILLED
I WASH MY HANDS OF THIS MATTER— I AM INNOCENT OF THE BLOOD OF THIS JUST PERSON!
RELEASE BARABBAS!

ALL RIGHT, I WILL RELEASE BARABBAS —DO WITH JESUS AS YOU WISH — YOU CRUCIFY HIM, I FIND NO FAULT WITH THIS MAN!
THERE IS A SCARLET ROBE, KING— AND A CROWN OF THORNS AND A REED FOR A SCEPTRE!
I'LL SPIT ON HIM!
HE SAYS HE IS THE SON OF GOD AND BY OUR LAW HE SHOULD DIE!

PILATE, THOROUGHLY FRIGHTENED WHEN HE HEARS JESUS CALLED THE SON OF GOD, QUESTIONS HIM AGAIN ///
WHO ARE YOU? DON'T YOU KNOW I HAVE THE POWER TO RELEASE OR TO CRUCIFY YOU? ANSWER ME!
THOU COULDST HAVE NO POWER AT ALL AGAINST ME, EXCEPT IT WERE GIVEN THEE FROM ABOVE!

HE SAYS HE, NOT CAESAR, IS KING!
IF YOU LET THIS MAN GO, YOU'RE NOT CAESAR'S FRIEND!

PILATE, WORRIED THAT HE WOULD GET IN TO TROUBLE WITH HIS EMPEROR, IN ROME, GIVES IN TO THE MOB ////
SHALL I CRUCIFY YOUR KING?
WE HAVE NO KING BUT CAESAR!
AWAY WITH HIM!
AND SO THE ROMAN SOLDIERS, UPON ORDERS FROM PILATE, LEAD JESUS AWAY TO CRUCIFY HIM /////

Matthew 27:3-10, 27:32, Mark 15:21, Luke 23:26-30, John 19:17

Matthew 27:33-49, Mark 15:22-36, Luke 23:32-45, John 19:17-29

Matthew 27:50-56, Mark 15:37-41, Luke 23:46-49, John 19:30-37

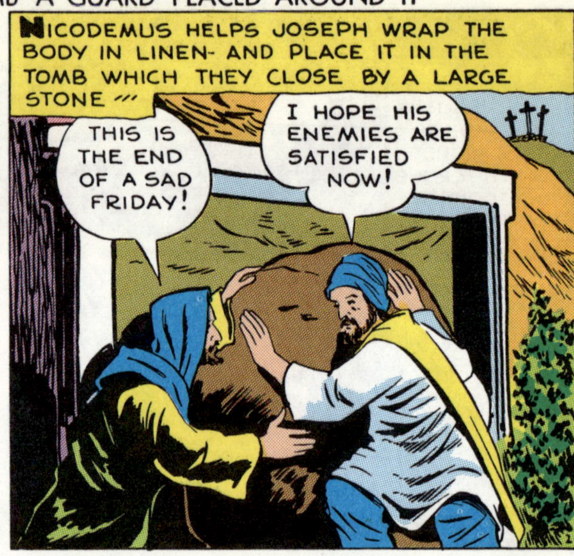

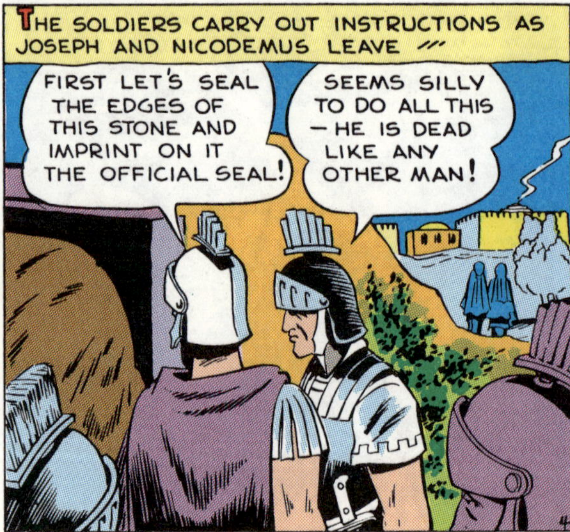

Matthew 27:57-66, Mark 15:42-46, Luke 23:50-54, John 19:38-42

Matthew 28:1-10, Mark 15:47, 16:1-11, Luke 23:55-56, 24:1-12 John 20:1-18

Matthew 28:11-15, Mark 16:12-13, Luke 24:13-35

Matthew 28:16, Mark 16:14, Luke 24:36-43, John 20:19-29

THEY FISH ALL NIGHT AND CATCH NOTHING
THERE IS SOME ONE ON THE SHORE SPEAKING TO US!
CAST THE NET ON THE RIGHT SIDE OF THE BOAT AND YE SHALL FIND!

THEY OBEY AND NOW THEY ARE HARDLY ABLE TO DRAW IN THE NET BECAUSE OF SO MANY FISH ~~~
IT'S OUR MASTER, PETER!
THEN I'M GOING ASHORE TO GREET HIM!

DISCIPLES IN ANOTHER SHIP ARE ASKED TO HELP DRAW THE NET TO LAND ~~~
HOW MANY DID WE CATCH?
I'VE JUST COUNTED, ONE HUNDRED AND FIFTY THREE!
YES, AND OUR NET DID NOT BREAK!

WITH PLENTY OF FISH THEY ALL DINE AROUND THE FIRE — JESUS SERVES THEM ~~~
COME AND DINE!
SEEMS GOOD FOR ALL OF US TO BE TOGETHER AGAIN!
THIS IS THE THIRD TIME JESUS HAS BEEN WITH US SINCE HE AROSE!

AFTER THEY HAD DINED, JESUS ASKS PETER THREE TIMES, IF HE LOVES HIM ~~~
MASTER, YOU KNOW ALL THINGS AND YOU KNOW I LOVE YOU!
FOLLOW ME AND FEED MY SHEEP!

SO FOR FORTY DAYS AFTER HIS RESURRECTION, JESUS MEETS WITH HIS DISCIPLES AND TEACHES THEM ABOUT HIS KINGDOM — ONE DAY HE ASKS THAT THEY MEET HIM ON A MOUNTAIN IN GALILLEE ~~~
ALL THINGS MUST BE FULFILLED, WHICH WERE WRITTEN IN THE LAW OF MOSES, IN THE PROPHETS AND IN THE PSALMS CONCERNING ME!

John 21:1-17

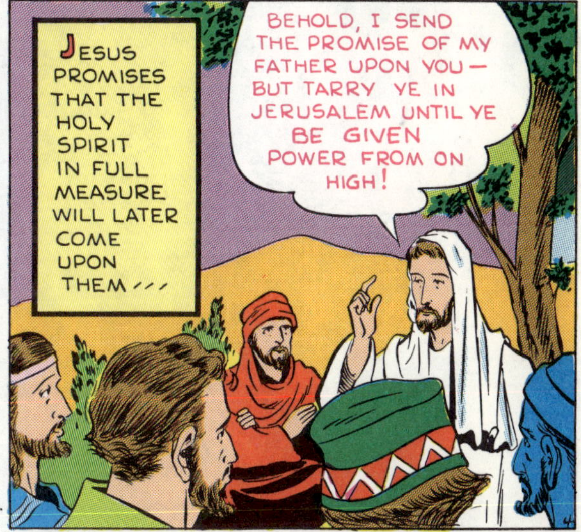

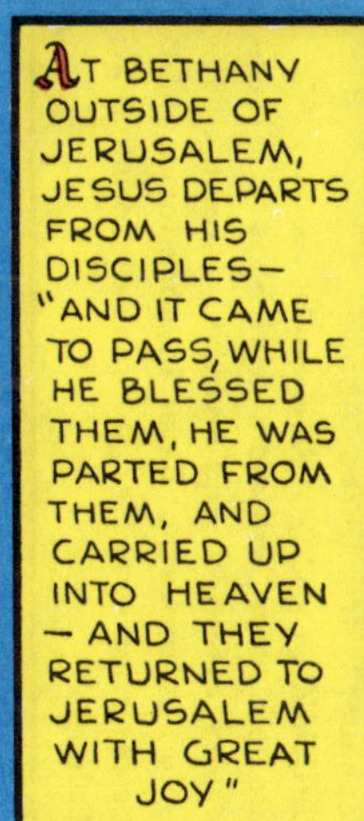

Matthew 28:17-20, Mark 16:15-20, Luke 24:44-53, John 20:30-31

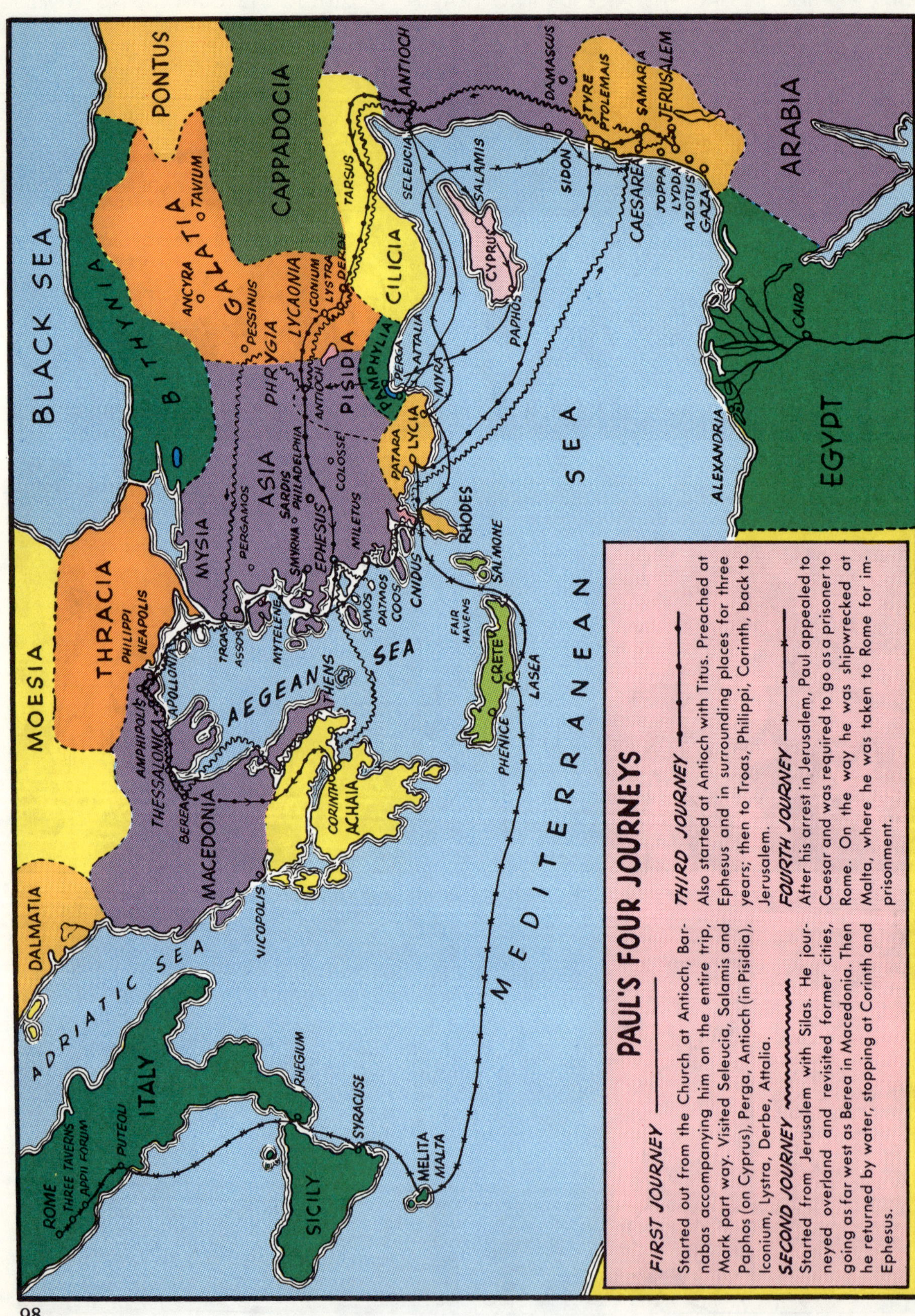

PAUL'S FOUR JOURNEYS

FIRST JOURNEY
Started out from the Church at Antioch, Barnabas accompanying him on the entire trip, Mark part way. Visited Seleucia, Salamis and Paphos (on Cyprus), Perga, Antioch (in Pisidia), Iconium, Lystra, Derbe, Attalia.

SECOND JOURNEY
Started from Jerusalem with Silas. He journeyed overland and revisited former cities, going as far west as Berea in Macedonia. Then he returned by water, stopping at Corinth and Ephesus.

THIRD JOURNEY
Also started at Antioch with Titus. Preached at Ephesus and in surrounding places for three years; then to Troas, Philippi, Corinth, back to Jerusalem.

FOURTH JOURNEY
After his arrest in Jerusalem, Paul appealed to Caesar and was required to go as a prisoner to Rome. On the way he was shipwrecked at Malta, where he was taken to Rome for imprisonment.

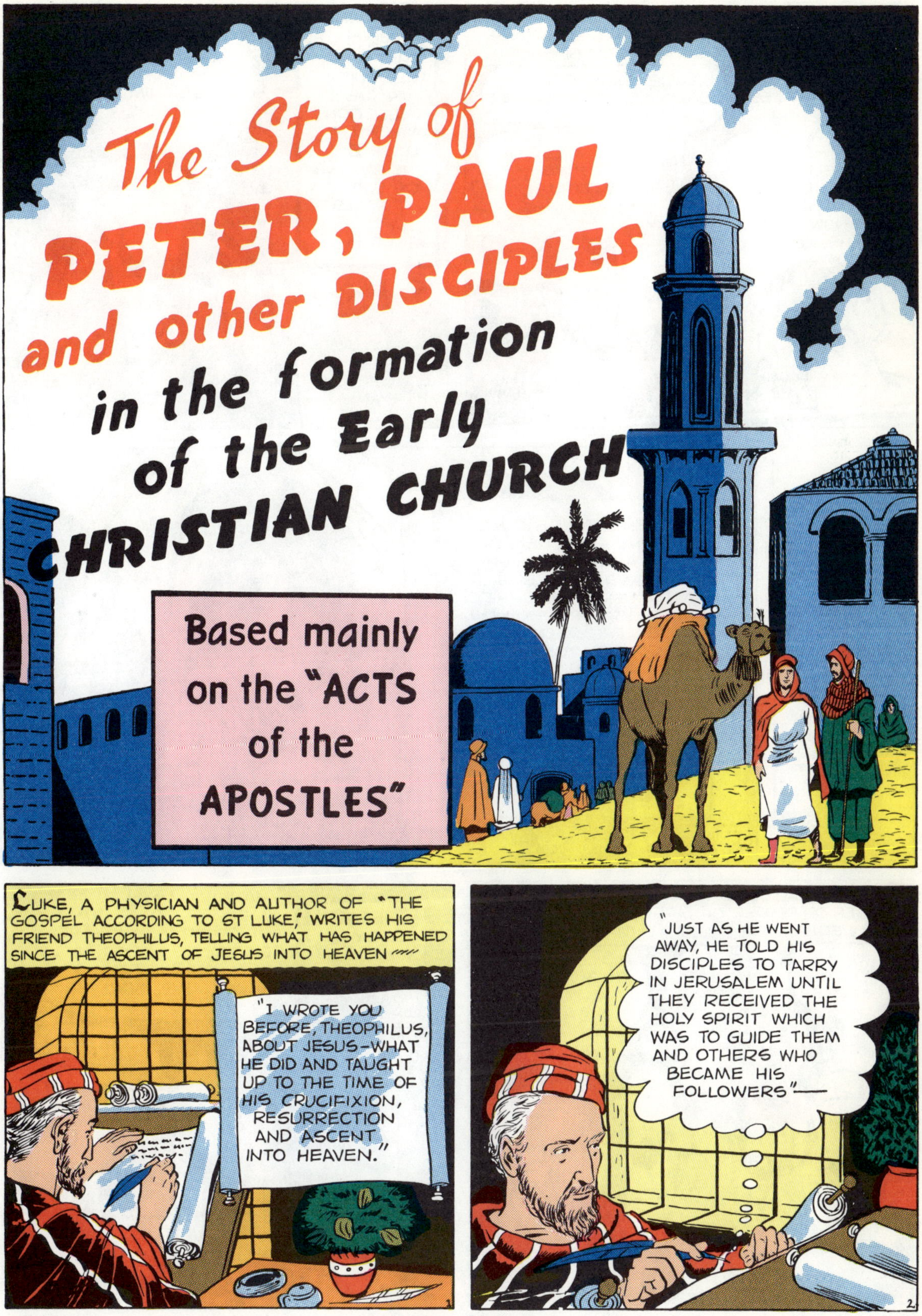

The Story of PETER, PAUL and other DISCIPLES

in the formation of the Early CHRISTIAN CHURCH

Based mainly on the "ACTS of the APOSTLES"

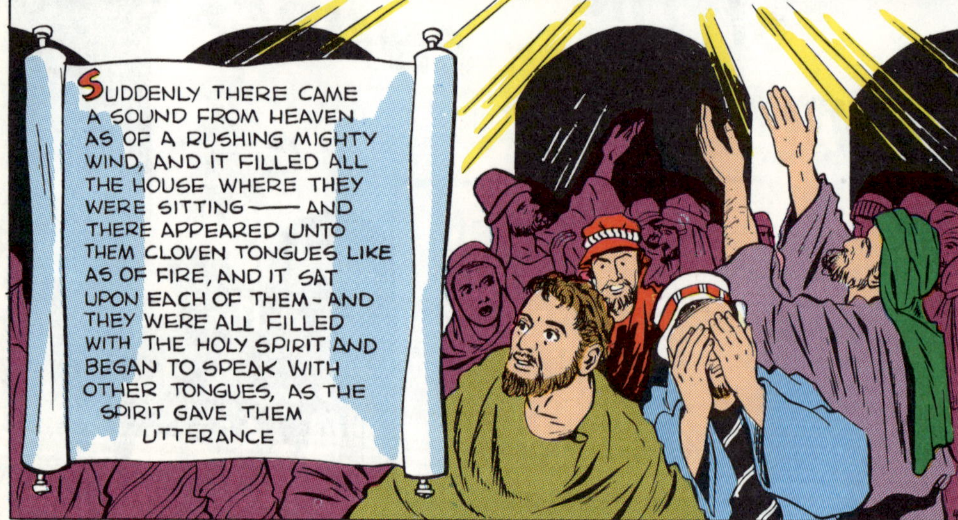

Acts 1:12-26; Acts 2:1-15

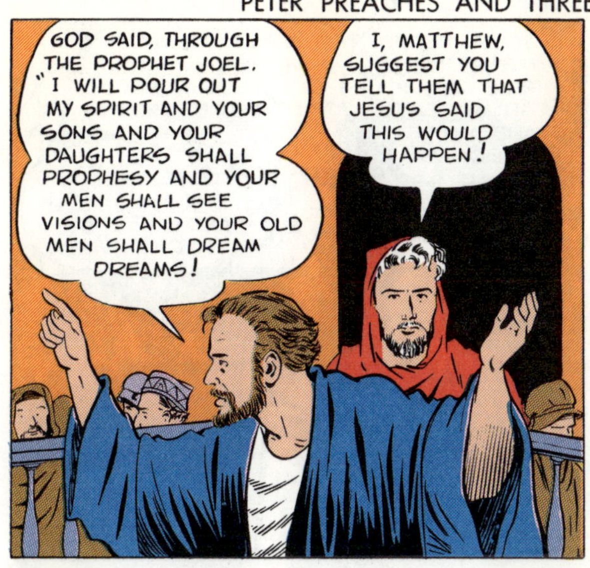
GOD SAID, THROUGH THE PROPHET JOEL, "I WILL POUR OUT MY SPIRIT AND YOUR SONS AND YOUR DAUGHTERS SHALL PROPHESY AND YOUR MEN SHALL SEE VISIONS AND YOUR OLD MEN SHALL DREAM DREAMS!
I, MATTHEW, SUGGEST YOU TELL THEM THAT JESUS SAID THIS WOULD HAPPEN!

YES, JESUS SHOWED BY SIGNS AND MIRACLES THAT HE CAME FROM GOD— THE ROMAN EMPEROR HAD HIM CRUCIFIED, BUT GOD RAISED HIM FROM THE DEAD AS YOUR PATRIARCH DAVID HAD PROPHESIED —HE LIVES TODAY IN OUR HEARTS, BY HIS SPIRIT!
THAT'S ALL TOO TRUE!
WHAT SHALL WE DO TO RECEIVE HIM AND HIS SPIRIT!

REPENT AND BE BAPTIZED IN THE NAME OF JESUS CHRIST FOR YOUR SINS AND YOU TOO, WILL RECEIVE THE GIFT OF THE HOLY SPIRIT!

AS A RESULT OF PETER'S TALK SOME 3000 PEOPLE, IN ONE DAY, BECOME DISCIPLES OF JESUS—
NOW WE KNOW THAT WHAT WE SAW AND HEARD WAS REAL!
I'M SURE TOO SINCE I WAS BAPTIZED!
WE ALL SEEM LIKE BROTHERS AND SISTERS —WE'LL SHARE TOGETHER ALL OUR POSSESSIONS!

AND THEY, CONTINUING DAILY WITH ONE ACCORD IN THE TEMPLE, AND BREAKING BREAD FROM HOUSE TO HOUSE, DID EAT THEIR MEAT WITH GLADNESS AND SINGLENESS OF HEART, PRAISING GOD, AND HAVING FAVOR WITH ALL THE PEOPLE. —AND THE LORD ADDED TO THE CHURCH DAILY SUCH AS SHOULD BE SAVED."

Acts 3:1-26; Acts 4:1-12

WITH PETER, JOHN AND THE BEGGAR OUT OF THE ROOM, THE RELIGIOUS LEADERS CONFER ~~~
WHAT SHALL WE DO WITH THESE MEN?
THEY HAVE HEALED THE LAME BEGGER, WE CAN'T DENY THAT!
YES AND WE NEED TO BE CAREFUL — THOUSANDS NOW BELIEVE WHAT PETER PREACHES!

THE THREE ARE WARNED NOT TO PREACH ABOUT JESUS ~~~
WE'VE DECIDED NOT TO PUNISH YOU, BUT HENCEFORTH YOU ARE NOT TO SPEAK OR TO TEACH IN THE NAME OF JESUS!
WHETHER IT BE RIGHT TO LISTEN TO YOU OR TO GOD, DECIDE FOR YOURSELVES!
WE CANNOT HELP SPEAK OF THINGS WHICH WE HAVE SEEN AND HEARD!

PETER AND JOHN RETURN TO THE COMPANY OF DISCIPLES ~~~
THEY SAID WE WERE NOT TO PREACH OR PERFORM ANY MIRACLES IN THE NAME OF JESUS!
THE HEALED BEGGAR WAS THERE AS EVIDENCE OF JESUS' POWER. THEY COULD SAY NOTHING!

THE DISCIPLES HOLD A PRAYER MEETING PRAISING GOD
LORD, THOU ART GOD! — BEHOLD THE THREATENING MADE TO PETER AND JOHN — GRANT UNTO THEM BOLDNESS THAT THEY MAY CONTINUE TO SPEAK!

AGAIN THERE WAS A SIGN OF THE HOLY SPIRIT IN THEIR MIDST ~~~
WITH ADDITIONAL ASSURANCE OF THE HOLY SPIRIT WE WILL NEVER CEASE TO PROCLAIM CHRIST AND HIS RESURRECTION!

THESE EARLY DISCIPLES IN THEIR UNSELFISH- NESS SOLD THEIR POSSESSIONS AND BROUGHT THE PROCEEDS TO HELP ALL ~~~
I AM JOSES, FROM CYPRESS — I HAVE SOLD MY LAND AND HERE IS MY PART FOR THE FUND!

"BUT A CERTAIN MAN NAMED ANANIAS WITH SAPPHIRA HIS WIFE, SOLD A POSSESSION"
YES, I GOT A GOOD PRICE FOR THE LAND— WE'LL KEEP PART OF THE MONEY AND TURN OVER THE BALANCE, SAYING THAT WE ARE GIVING ALL!
IT'S A LARGE SUM ANYWAY —THEY WILL THINK US GENEROUS!

ANANIAS BRINGS HIS GIFT TO PETER ～～
I SOLD MY LAND. MY WIFE AND I DECIDED TO GIVE ALL THE MONEY TO THE COMMON FUND!
WHY DO YOU LISTEN TO SATAN AND LIE TO THE HOLY SPIRIT? THE MONEY WAS YOURS TO DO WITH AS YOU WISHED—YOU HAVE NOT LIED TO MAN BUT TO GOD!

ANANIAS IS PUNISHED FOR HIS LYING ～～
LOOK! ANANIAS HAS FAINTED!
NO, HE IS DEAD-CARRY OUT HIS BODY AND BURY IT!

THREE HOURS LATER SAPPHIRA COMES IN, NOT KNOWING WHAT HAS HAPPENED ～～
TELL ME, DID YOU SELL YOUR PROPERTY TO GIVE TO THE FUND?
YES, MY HUSBAND BROUGHT ALL THE MONEY TO YOU!

WHY DID YOU AND ANANIAS DECIDE TOGETHER TO TEMPT THE SPIRIT OF GOD? THE YOUNG MEN WHO CARRIED OUT YOUR DEAD HUSBAND ARE AT THE DOOR!
DEAD DID YOU SAY? I CAN'T STAND THIS!

SAPPHIRA ALSO DIES!
SHE WAS PUNISHED TOO FOR TELLING A FALSEHOOD!
AND GREAT FEAR CAME UPON ALL THE CHURCH AND UPON AS MANY AS HEARD THESE THINGS

CROWDS FROM JERUSALEM AND TOWNS AROUND, BRING THEIR SICK TO PETER AND THE OTHER DISCIPLES, TO BE HEALED ~~~
HOPE PETER WILL COME ALONG SOON AND HEAL MY WIFE!
PERHAPS PETER'S SHADOW WILL FALL ON MY LITTLE BOY —SOME HAVE BEEN CURED EVEN THAT WAY!

BECAUSE OF THE INCREASING NUMBER OF BELIEVERS, PETER'S OPPONENTS BECAME INDIGNANT — THEY ARREST PETER WITH SOME OTHER DISCIPLES AND PUT THEM IN PRISON ~~~
I'VE JUST HAD A VISION— AN ANGEL TOLD ME THAT OUT THAT WAY IS AN OPEN DOOR— LET'S GO!

THEY CALL A COUNCIL AND SEND FOR THE DISCIPLES IN THE PRISON ~~~
WHY HAVE YOU NOT BROUGHT THE PRISONERS?
SIRE, THEY WERE NOT IN THE PRISON!
THEY HAVE ESCAPED AND ARE PREACHING AGAIN IN THE TEMPLE!

PETER AND HIS ASSOCIATES ARE BROUGHT BEFORE THE COUNCIL ~~~
DID WE NOT FORBID YOU TO TALK TO THE CROWD ABOUT JESUS? YOU'VE FILLED JERUSALEM WITH HIS TEACHINGS!
WE PROPOSE TO OBEY GOD RATHER THAN MAN!
YES, WE WILL BEAR WITNESS TO JESUS AND TO THE HOLY SPIRIT WHOM GOD GIVES TO ALL WHO OBEY HIM!

THE RELIGIOUS AUTHORITIES HOLD A PRIVATE COUNCIL — GAMALIEL, A NOTED DOCTOR OF LAW, CAUTIONS THEM ~~~
SOME OF YOU WANT TO STOP THIS TEACHING —IF THIS IS FROM GOD YOU CAN'T STOP IT —IF IT IS FROM MAN IT WILL FAIL IN TIME, AS OTHER UPRISINGS!

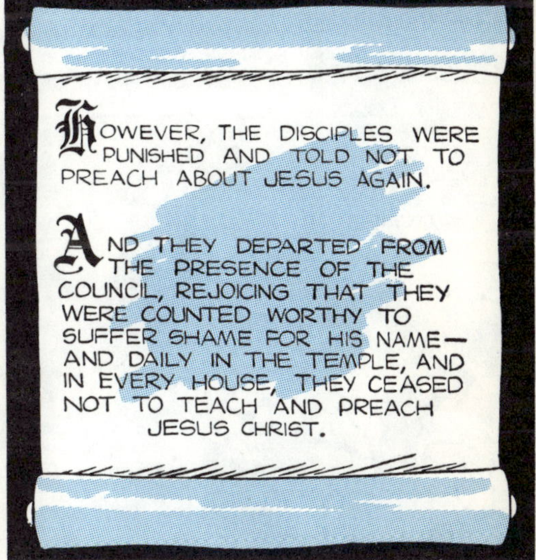
HOWEVER, THE DISCIPLES WERE PUNISHED AND TOLD NOT TO PREACH ABOUT JESUS AGAIN.
AND THEY DEPARTED FROM THE PRESENCE OF THE COUNCIL, REJOICING THAT THEY WERE COUNTED WORTHY TO SUFFER SHAME FOR HIS NAME — AND DAILY IN THE TEMPLE, AND IN EVERY HOUSE, THEY CEASED NOT TO TEACH AND PREACH JESUS CHRIST.

STEPHEN DEFENDS HIMSELF IN A LONG ADDRESS— HE SAYS THAT JESUS' TEACHINGS ARE NOT CONTRARY TO MOSES—THAT THEY ONLY MAKE THEM CLEARER ~~~

Acts 6:1-15, Acts 7:1-60

ANTAGONISM TOWARD THE DISCIPLES IN JERUSALEM BEGINS—SAUL TAKES A LEADING PART~~~
I, SAUL OF TARSUS, WOULD LIKE TO JOIN WITH YOU IN STAMPING OUT THIS FOOLISH RELIGION—GIVE ME A LETTER OF AUTHORITY!
HERE, GO AFTER THEM, HURRY, SEEK THEM OUT IN THEIR HOMES AND PUT THEM IN PRISON!

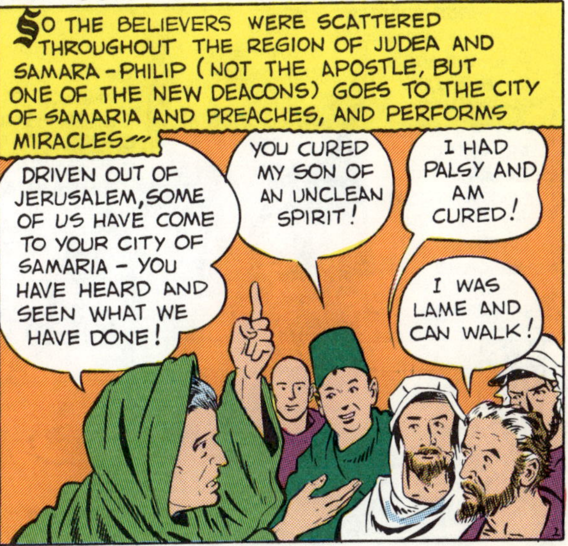
SO THE BELIEVERS WERE SCATTERED THROUGHOUT THE REGION OF JUDEA AND SAMARA—PHILIP (NOT THE APOSTLE, BUT ONE OF THE NEW DEACONS) GOES TO THE CITY OF SAMARIA AND PREACHES, AND PERFORMS MIRACLES~~~
DRIVEN OUT OF JERUSALEM, SOME OF US HAVE COME TO YOUR CITY OF SAMARIA—YOU HAVE HEARD AND SEEN WHAT WE HAVE DONE!
YOU CURED MY SON OF AN UNCLEAN SPIRIT!
I HAD PALSY AND AM CURED!
I WAS LAME AND CAN WALK!

"THERE WAS A CERTAIN MAN CALLED SIMON.. WHO USED SORCERY AND BEWITCHED THE PEOPLE... STATING THAT HE HIMSELF WAS SOME GREAT ONE TO WHOM THEY ALL GAVE HEED... SAYING "THIS MAN IS THE GREAT POWER OF GOD."
I'D LIKE TO DO MIRACLES TOO LIKE YOU—I NOW AM A BAPTISED BELIEVER!

WHEN THE DISCIPLES WHO REMAINED AT JERUSALEM HEARD OF THE LARGE NUMBER IN SAMARIA BECOMING FOLLOWERS THEY DECIDED TO SEND PETER AND JOHN TO HELP PHILIP~~~
NEVER COULD I PERFORM SUCH WONDERFUL THINGS—HERE, PETER, IS SOME MONEY, GIVE ME THIS POWER!
LET YOUR MONEY PERISH WITH YOU!—AS THOUGH THE GIFT OF GOD CAN BE PURCHASED—YOUR HEART IS NOT RIGHT IN THE SIGHT OF GOD—REPENT OF YOUR WICKEDNESS AND PRAY AND PERHAPS GOD MAY FORGIVE YOU!

OH PRAY TO THE LORD FOR ME THAT NONE OF THESE THINGS COME UPON ME!

PETER AND JOHN, AFTER THEY PREACHED IN SAMARIA AND THE SURROUNDING TOWNS, RETURN AGAIN TO JERUSALEM~~~
STRANGE EXPERIENCES WE HAVE HAD!
PEOPLE GET THE WRONG IDEA OF WHAT GOD WANTS, NOT MIRACLES BUT RIGHT LIVING!

"AND THE ANGEL OF THE LORD SPAKE UNTO PHILIP, SAYING, ARISE GO TOWARD THE SOUTH...FROM JERUSALEM UNTO GAZA. WHICH IS DESERT"
HELLO, STRANGER! RETURNING FROM JERUSALEM?
I'M GOING BACK TO ETHIOPIA—I'M AN OFFICIAL UNDER CANDACE THE QUEEN — I HAVING CHARGE OF HER TREASURES — COME UP AND RIDE!

YOU ARE READING FROM THE PROPHET ISAIAH— DO YOU UNDERSTAND WHAT YOU ARE READING?
HOW CAN I, EXCEPT SOME ONE EXPLAINS —HERE IN THE FIFTY THIRD CHAPTER OF ISAIAH IS HE SPEAKING OF HIMSELF?

"HE WAS LED AS A SHEEP TO THE SLAUGHTER; AND LIKE A LAMB DUMB BEFORE HIS SHEARER SO OPENED HE NOT HIS MOUTH: IN HIS HUMILIATION HIS JUDGMENT WAS TAKEN AWAY: AND WHO SHALL DECLARE HIS GENERATION? FOR HIS LIFE IS TAKEN FROM THE EARTH"

PHILIP EXPLAINS HOW ISAIAH, YEARS BEFORE, FORETELLS OF JESUS ~~~
IT IS TO JESUS THAT THE PROPHET REFERS —IT IS OF HIM YOU HEARD IN JERUSALEM —HE CAME TO GIVE TRUE LIFE TO AS MANY AS BELIEVE AND ARE BAPTIZED!

AND SO THE ETHIOPIAN IS BAPTIZED AND BECOMES A CHRISTIAN ~~~
HERE IS WATER. WHAT IS TO HINDER ME FROM BEING BAPTIZED?
IF YOU BELIEVE WITH ALL YOUR HEART YOU MAY!

I TRULY BELIEVE THAT JESUS IS THE SON OF GOD!
MAY GOD USE YOU IN ETHIOPIA TO PREACH HIM THERE AMONG YOUR PEOPLE!
PHILIP LEAVES HIM WHILE THE ETHIOPIAN GOES HAPPILY ON HIS WAY ~~~

Acts 8:26-40

SAUL, MEANWHILE, DETERMINED TO ARREST THE CHRISTIANS, JOURNEYS TOWARD DAMASCUS— SUDDENLY THERE BURST UPON HIM A BLINDING LIGHT AND A VOICE FROM HEAVEN ~~~
SAUL, SAUL, WHY PERSECUTEST THOU ME?
WHO ART THOU, LORD?

IT IS JESUS WHO SPEAKS TO SAUL ~~~
LORD, WHAT DO YOU WANT ME TO DO?
I AM JESUS WHOM THOU PERSECUTEST ~~ ARISE ~~ GO INTO THE CITY ~~~ IT SHALL BE TOLD THEE, WHAT THOU MUST DO!

SAUL, BLINDED, IS LED ALONG THE ROAD TO DAMASCUS
I KNOW A MAN IN DAMASCUS CALLED JUDAS WHO LIVES ON STRAIGHT STREET — HE'LL GIVE US FOOD AND LODGING!
I CAN'T SEE A THING — HOPE I AM NOT PERMANENTLY BLIND!

IN ANOTHER PART OF DAMASCUS, JESUS APPEARS IN A VISION TO A DISCIPLE NAMED ANANIAS ~~~
ARISE AND GO TO THE HOUSE OF JUDAS AND INQUIRE FOR ONE, SAUL OF TARSUS, FOR HE PRAYETH!
LORD, I HAVE HEARD HOW SAUL, WITH AUTHORITY FROM THE HIGH PRIESTS, IS ARRESTING ALL WHO CALL ON YOUR NAME!

UPON A FURTHER COMMAND ANANIAS GOES TO VISIT SAUL ~~~
GO THY WAY FOR SAUL IS A CHOSEN VESSEL UNTO ME TO BEAR MY NAME BEFORE THE GENTILES AND KINGS AND THE CHILDREN OF ISRAEL!

SAUL HAS HIS SIGHT RESTORED UPON ANANIAS' VISIT ~~~
BROTHER SAUL, THE LORD, EVEN JESUS SENT ME THAT YOU MIGHT RECEIVE YOUR SIGHT AND THE POWER OF THE HOLY SPIRIT!
OH, I CAN SEE NOW AND I FEEL GOD'S POWER — I WILL OBEY HIS COMMANDS!
HE MUST EAT SOMETHING — HE'S BEEN WITHOUT FOOD OR DRINK FOR THREE DAYS!

AFTER A LONG PERIOD OF MEDITATION IN THE DESERT, SAUL RETURNS TO DAMASCUS, A CHRISTIAN ---
CAN IT BE THAT SAUL, THE PERSECUTER, IS NOW ONE OF US?
HE HAS BEEN BAPTIZED AND IS ALREADY PREACHING CHRIST IN OUR SYNAGOGUES!

SAUL DOES NOT HAVE AN EASY TIME OF IT — HIS FORMER COMPANIONS BEGIN CONSPIRING AGAINST HIM ---
LET'S WATCH THE TWO GATES OUT OF DAMASCUS AND GET SAUL WHEN HE TRIES TO LEAVE!
YES, LET'S STRIKE HIM DOWN FOR DESERTING US AND THE PRIESTS!

BUT SAUL'S FRIENDS HELP HIM TO ESCAPE BY LOWERING HIM IN A BASKET FROM THE CITY WALL ---
BROTHER BARNABAS HAS JUST GIVEN THE SIGNAL TO LET YOU DOWN — HE'LL GO WITH YOU TO JERUSALEM!
GOD BLESS YOU AND KEEP YOU SAFE!

SAUL AND BARNABAS REACH JERUSALEM — BUT ALL THE DISCIPLES THERE MISTRUST SAUL ---
PERHAPS THIS IS SAUL'S TRICK TO LEARN ABOUT US AND THEN ARREST US!
LET'S ASK BARNABAS — HE KNOWS!

BARNABAS EXPLAINS TO THE DISCIPLES HOW SAUL WAS CONVERTED
A REMARKABLE THING HAPPENED! — JESUS APPEARED TO SAUL ON HIS WAY TO DAMASCUS WHERE HE PLANNED TO PERSECUTE US CHRISTIANS — BUT NOW HE IS CONVERTED AND TELLS EVERY ONE ABOUT CHRIST!

AS SAUL PREACHES TO THE GREEKS IN JERUSALEM, HIS ENEMIES PLAN AGAIN TO SEIZE HIM ---
WHEN HE GETS THROUGH LET'S GRAB HIM AND TAKE HIM TO THE AUTHORITIES!
YES, HE IS A TRAITOR!

Acts 9:20-29

WITH THE DANGER TO SAUL'S LIFE INCREASING, HIS JERUSALEM FRIENDS DECIDE TO SEND HIM TO HIS HOME CITY OF TARSUS ~~~
HERE FROM CAESAREA YOU WILL GO BY BOAT TO TARSUS — AFTER THE TROUBLE BLOWS OVER, I'LL SEND OR COME FOR YOU!
YES, BETTER REST UP AND STAY AWAY FOR A WHILE!

"THEN HAD THE CHURCHES REST THROUGHOUT ALL JUDEA AND GALILEE AND SAMARIA, AND WERE EDIFIED, AND WALKING IN THE FEAR OF THE LORD, AND IN THE COMFORT OF THE HOLY SPIRIT, WERE MULTIPLIED"

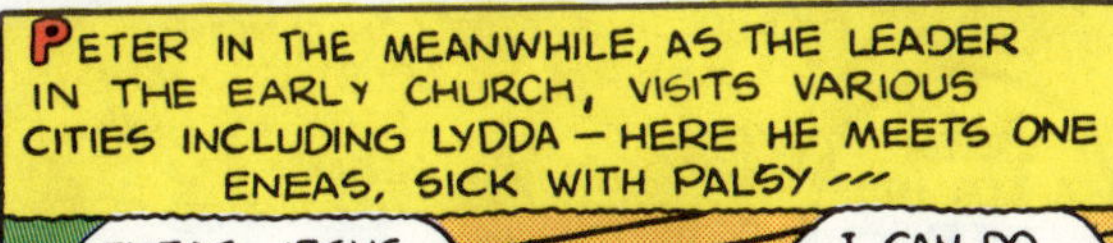

PETER IN THE MEANWHILE, AS THE LEADER IN THE EARLY CHURCH, VISITS VARIOUS CITIES INCLUDING LYDDA — HERE HE MEETS ONE ENEAS, SICK WITH PALSY ~~~
ENEAS, JESUS CHRIST WILL MAKE YOU WHOLE — ARISE AND WALK!
I CAN DO IT! SEE I'M STANDING UP, THE FIRST TIME IN EIGHT YEARS!

WHEN ALL THE PEOPLE OF LYDDA AND THE ADJOINING TOWN OF SARON SEE AND HEAR THIS CURED MAN, THEY BECOME BELIEVERS ~~~
WHAT JESUS CHRIST HAS DONE FOR AENEAS HE CAN DO FOR YOU!
JESUS NOT ONLY CURED ME BUT FORGAVE MY SINS!

WHILE PREACHING AT LYDDA. PETER IS SUMMONED TO JOPPA A NEARBY TOWN ~~~
DORCAS, A DEVOUT CHRISTIAN WOMAN CALLED TABITHA, HAS DIED — THE DISCIPLES ASK THAT YOU COME AND COMFORT THEM!
I'LL GO WITH YOU AT ONCE!

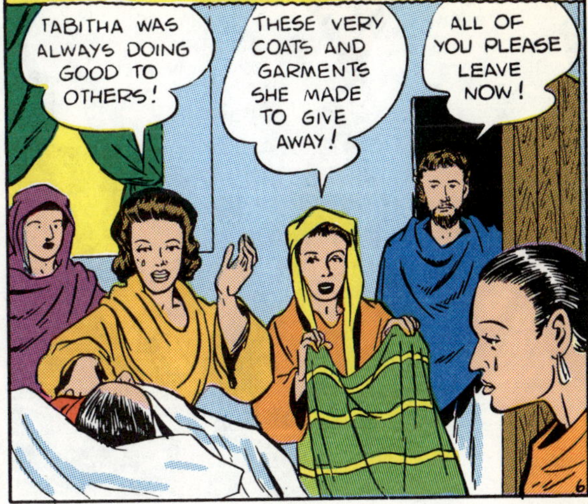
IN DORCAS' HOUSE PETER FINDS HER FRIENDS WEEPING ~~~
TABITHA WAS ALWAYS DOING GOOD TO OTHERS!
THESE VERY COATS AND GARMENTS SHE MADE TO GIVE AWAY!
ALL OF YOU PLEASE LEAVE NOW!

PETER PRAYS BY THE BEDSIDE OF DORCAS ~~
OH, GOD IF IT IS THY WILL THOU HAST THE POWER, EVEN TO RAISE THIS WOMAN TO LIFE!

PETER, CALLING HER BY HER GIVEN NAME, TELLS HER TO GET UP ~~
TABITHA, ARISE!

"AND SHE OPENED HER EYES AND WHEN SHE SAW PETER, SHE SAT UP"
HERE, TAKE MY HAND —JESUS CHRIST HAS HEALED YOU!
PETER, THIS IS A MIRACLE —I'VE BEEN BROUGHT BACK FROM THE DEAD!

PETER CALLS IN HER FRIENDS
HERE IS ANOTHER SIGN OF GOD'S AMAZING POWER WORKING AMONG US!
CAN ANYONE DOUBT GOD NOW, AFTER WE HAVE SEEN HER RESTORED?
WE SHOULD ALL GIVE PRAISE TO GOD!

THE NEWS SPREAD ALL OVER JOPPA AND MANY CAME TO BELIEVE IN GOD ~~
WE KNOW DORCAS—SHE DESERVES TO LIVE MANY MORE YEARS!
I'M CONVINCED BY ALL THIS —I TOO NOW WILL BECOME A CHRISTIAN!

SIMON, A TANNER IN JOPPA, INVITES PETER TO STAY AT HIS HOME ~~
YOU ARE A BLESSING TO OUR CITY —COME AND STAY WITH ME!
I'LL GLADLY DO SO—WITH SO MANY NEW BELIEVERS THERE'S MUCH TO DO!

Acts 9:40-43

A ROMAN CENTURION NAMED CORNELIUS, LIVING IN CAESAREA, WAS AT PRAYER ONE AFTERNOON, WHEN IN A VISION, AN ANGEL APPEARS ---
WHAT IS IT YOU WANT?
CORNELIUS, YOUR PRAYERS AND GENEROUS GIFTS HAVE COME UP AS A MEMORIAL TO GOD - SEND TO JOPPA AND ASK FOR ONE, PETER, TO COME HERE TO YOUR HOME!

CORNELIUS DISPATCHES TWO SERVANTS AND A SOLDIER TO BRING PETER ---
GO TO JOPPA, FIND PETER, AS THE ANGEL HAS SAID, AND ASK HIM TO COME HERE!
WE'LL TELL HIM ALL THAT HAPPENED!

THE NEXT DAY AROUND NOON THE MEN ARRIVED AT JOPPA - PETER IS PRAYING AND RESTING ON THE HOUSE TOP ---
I WISH MY FRIENDS WOULD HURRY WITH DINNER - I'M DROWSY, I'LL TAKE A LITTLE NAP!

PETER HAS A STRANGE DREAM - A SHEET IS LET DOWN FROM HEAVEN BY FOUR CORNERS - - IN IT ARE ALL MANNER OF WILD ANIMALS, CREEPING THINGS AND BIRDS ---
RISE, PETER, KILL AND EAT!
NOT SO, LORD - I'VE NEVER EATEN ANYTHING WHICH IS COMMON OR UNCLEAN!

PETER IS PERPLEXED, BECAUSE AS A DEVOUT JEW, HE OBSERVED STRICTLY THE JEWISH DIETARY LAWS ---
WHAT DOES ALL THIS MEAN?

WHILE PETER PONDERS ABOUT THESE THINGS, THE HOLY SPIRIT WITHIN TELLS HIM TO GO DOWNSTAIRS WHERE THE THREE MEN ARE NOW WAITING ---
I'M PETER WHOM YOU SEEK - WHAT DO YOU WANT?
WE COME FROM CORNELIUS THE CENTURION AT CAESAREA - HE HAD A VISION - AN ANGEL TOLD HIM TO SEND FOR YOU - HE DOES NOT UNDERSTAND AND WANTS YOU TO COME AND EXPLAIN!

SO PETER, CONVINCED THAT GOD HAS SOME PURPOSE IN THESE STRANGE HAPPENINGS, TAKES SOME FRIENDS AND GOES ALONG THE NEXT MORNING TO VISIT CORNELIUS

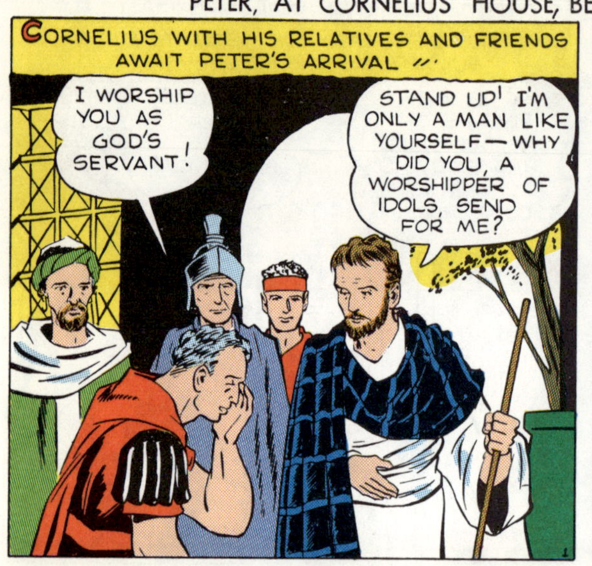
CORNELIUS WITH HIS RELATIVES AND FRIENDS AWAIT PETER'S ARRIVAL "
I WORSHIP YOU AS GOD'S SERVANT!
STAND UP! I'M ONLY A MAN LIKE YOURSELF — WHY DID YOU, A WORSHIPPER OF IDOLS, SEND FOR ME?

I CALLED FOR YOU TO EXPLAIN SOME MYSTERIOUS THINGS THAT HAPPENED— FOUR DAYS AGO, ABOUT THIS TIME, I WAS PRAYING, WHEN AN ANGEL APPEARED AND TOLD ME TO SEND FOR YOU!
WHILE WE HAVE BEEN INSTRUCTED TO PREACH TO THE HOUSE OF ISRAEL, GOD HAS DIRECTED ME HERE TO YOU!

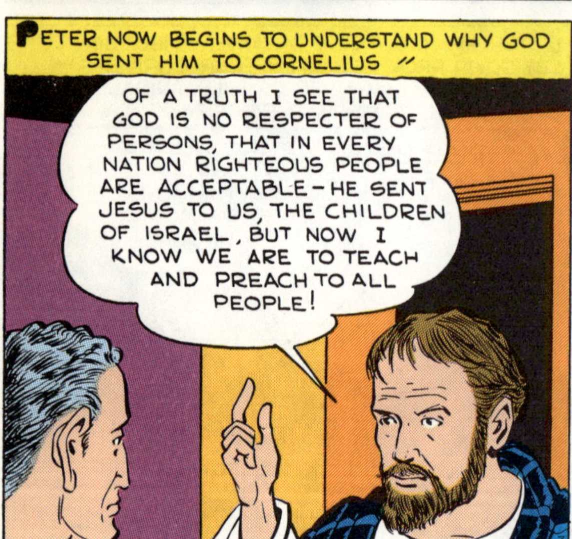
PETER NOW BEGINS TO UNDERSTAND WHY GOD SENT HIM TO CORNELIUS "
OF A TRUTH I SEE THAT GOD IS NO RESPECTER OF PERSONS, THAT IN EVERY NATION RIGHTEOUS PEOPLE ARE ACCEPTABLE — HE SENT JESUS TO US, THE CHILDREN OF ISRAEL, BUT NOW I KNOW WE ARE TO TEACH AND PREACH TO ALL PEOPLE!

AS PETER SPEAKS, THE HOLY SPIRIT COMES INTO THE HEARTS OF HIS LISTENERS "
PETER, WE NOW UNDERSTAND YOUR WORDS AND FEEL THE POWER OF THE HOLY SPIRIT!
PRAISE GOD! I KNOW JESUS FORGIVES MY SINS FOR HE GIVES ME PEACE!

ALL YOU WHO BELIEVE THAT JESUS IS THE SON OF GOD WILL BE BAPTIZED!
AFTER WHAT WE HAVE SEEN WE CANNOT DOUBT THAT THE GOSPEL IS FOR US TOO!

FROM NOW ON ALL BELIEVERS, NOT ONLY JEWS, BUT ALSO GENTILES, ARE BAPTIZED "
NOW YOU HAVE FULFILLED ALL THAT JESUS COMMANDS!
DO STAY WITH US AND TELL US MORE OF JESUS' WORDS!

Acts 10:24-48

PETER UPON RETURNING TO JERUSALEM IS ASKED TO EXPLAIN HIS CONDUCT —
YOU PREACHED TO THE GENTILES, WORSHIPPERS OF IDOLS—BY WHAT AUTHORITY?
I FELT IT WRONG TOO, UNTIL GOD IN A VISION MADE ME SEE DIFFERENTLY —IN A GREAT NET LET DOWN FROM HEAVEN I SAW ALL SORTS OF STRANGE ANIMALS AND BIRDS— I WAS TOLD TO 'SLAY AND EAT'— I REFUSED, SAYING THEY WERE UNCLEAN!

BUT PETER, WHAT HAS ALL THIS TO DO WITH PREACHING TO THE GENTILES?
I COULD NOT UNDERSTAND UNTIL CORNELIUS SENT FOR ME TO EXPLAIN HIS VISION — THEN WHEN I PREACHED JESUS, AND ALL ACCEPTED HIM, I UNDERSTOOD BOTH VISIONS, MINE AND HIS—THEY MEAN THE GOSPEL IS FOR JEW AND GENTILE ALIKE

THAT MAY BE ONLY YOUR IDEA — WHAT AUTHORITY HAVE YOU FROM JESUS?
I REMEMBER JESUS' WORDS—'JOHN INDEED BAPTIZED WITH WATER BUT YE SHALL BE BAPTIZED WITH THE HOLY SPIRIT'— IF GOD GAVE THESE GENTILES THE HOLY SPIRIT, WHO AM I THAT I SHOULD WITHSTAND GOD?

WHEN THEY HEARD THESE THINGS, THEY HELD THEIR PEACE AND GLORIFIED GOD, SAYING, 'THEN HATH GOD ALSO TO THE GENTILES, GRANTED REPENTANCE UNTO LIFE!

THE PERSECUTION OF JESUS' DISCIPLES AT THE TIME OF STEPHEN'S DEATH, SCATTERED THEM TO OTHER PLACES INCLUDING THE CITY OF ANTIOCH WHICH BECAME A LARGE COLONY OF BELIEVERS. BARNABAS IS SENT FROM JERUSALEM TO PREACH THERE —
I WANT TO SAY TO YOU GREEKS IN ANTIOCH THAT THE GOSPEL IS FOR YOU TOO — STAY CLOSE TO GOD — I REJOICE IN YOUR FAITH!

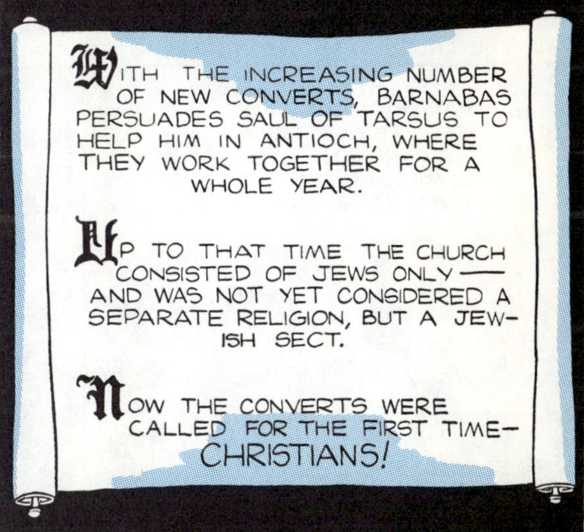
WITH THE INCREASING NUMBER OF NEW CONVERTS, BARNABAS PERSUADES SAUL OF TARSUS TO HELP HIM IN ANTIOCH, WHERE THEY WORK TOGETHER FOR A WHOLE YEAR.
UP TO THAT TIME THE CHURCH CONSISTED OF JEWS ONLY — AND WAS NOT YET CONSIDERED A SEPARATE RELIGION, BUT A JEWISH SECT.
NOW THE CONVERTS WERE CALLED FOR THE FIRST TIME— CHRISTIANS!

Acts 11:26-30; Acts 12:1-14

THE DISCIPLES CANNOT BELIEVE THAT PETER HAS ESCAPED !!!
I SAY PETER IS AT THE GATE—LISTEN, HEAR HIM KNOCKING?
IT'S IMPOSSIBLE —HE'S STILL IN PRISON!
SOMEONE IS KNOCKING —LET'S OPEN THE DOOR!

IT'S PETER ALL RIGHT!
BE QUIET AND I'LL TELL YOU HOW THE LORD DELIVERED ME!
WE SHOULD BE ASHAMED —WE PRAYED BUT REALLY DOUBTED THAT GOD WOULD DELIVER HIM!

KING HEROD SENDS OUT SOLDIERS TO RECAPTURE PETER WHO HAS ALREADY LEFT MARY'S HOUSE
WE'LL NEVER GET HIM—THE CHRISTIANS ARE HIDING HIM!
PETER IS WELL ON HIS WAY TO CAESARIA!
AT CAESARIA CORNELIUS WILL PROTECT HIM!

ABOUT THIS TIME THE PEOPLE OF TYRE AND SIDON, NEEDING FOOD, SEND MESSENGERS TO KING HEROD—THEY SPEAK TO BLASTUS THE KING'S CHAMBERLAIN !!!
BE A GOOD FRIEND AND ARRANGE FOR US TO SEE KING HEROD
SINCE YOUR COUNTRY IS NEXT TO HIS, HE WANTS PEACE!

ON AN APPOINTED DAY, KING HEROD IN ROYAL APPAREL GIVES AUDIENCE TO THEM !!!
YOU WANT FOOD AND PEACE — YOU KNOW HOW MIGHTY I AM — I'M IRRESISTIBLE!
HE SPEAKS LIKE A GOD, NOT A MAN!

"AND IMMEDIATELY THE ANGEL OF THE LORD SMOTE HIM, BECAUSE HE GAVE NOT GOD THE GLORY... BUT THE WORD OF GOD GREW AND MULTIPLIED"

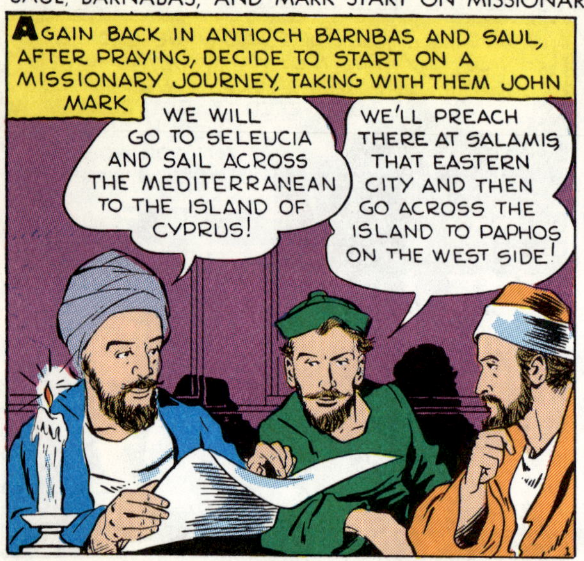

Acts 12:25; Acts 13:1-50

PAUL AND BARNABAS PREACH NEXT IN ICONIUM WHERE MANY BECOME BELIEVERS BUT TROUBLE STARTS
PAUL, OUR FRIENDS WARN THAT WE ARE TO BE STONED!
LET'S GO TO THE NEXT TOWN!

IN LYSTRA — A CRIPPLE LISTENS ATTENTIVELY TO PAUL
WITH FAITH IN JESUS, PERHAPS I TOO, CAN WALK AGAIN
YOU CAN DO IT! STAND UPRIGHT ON YOUR FEET!
HE HAS NEVER WALKED SINCE BIRTH!

THANK GOD! LOOK I CAN STAND AND EVEN WALK!
THOSE MEN ARE GODS COME DOWN AMONG US!

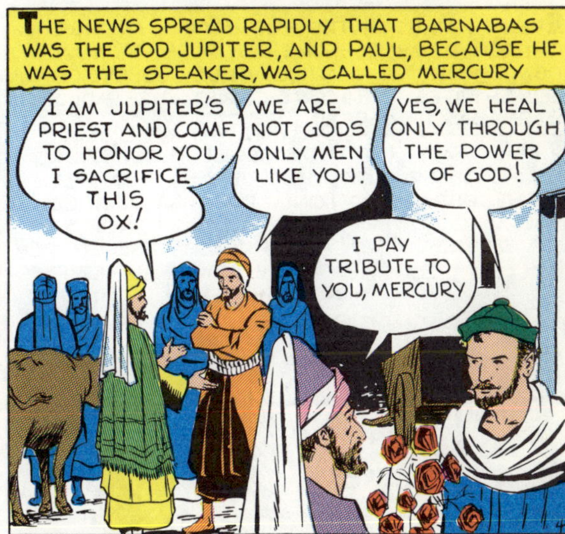
THE NEWS SPREAD RAPIDLY THAT BARNABAS WAS THE GOD JUPITER, AND PAUL, BECAUSE HE WAS THE SPEAKER, WAS CALLED MERCURY
I AM JUPITER'S PRIEST AND COME TO HONOR YOU. I SACRIFICE THIS OX!
WE ARE NOT GODS ONLY MEN LIKE YOU!
YES, WE HEAL ONLY THROUGH THE POWER OF GOD!
I PAY TRIBUTE TO YOU, MERCURY

IN THE MIDST OF THEIR GREAT POPULARITY, ENEMIES FROM ANTIOCH AND ICONIUM FOLLOW THEM AND STIR UP THE PEOPLE
WE ALMOST CAUGHT THEM BUT THEY RAN AWAY!
THEY WILL NOT ESCAPE US THIS TIME!

TROUBLE STARTS — PAUL IS HURT IN THE QUARREL
HE'S BEEN BADLY HURT!
LET'S HELP HIM!

Acts 14:20-28, Acts 15:1-29

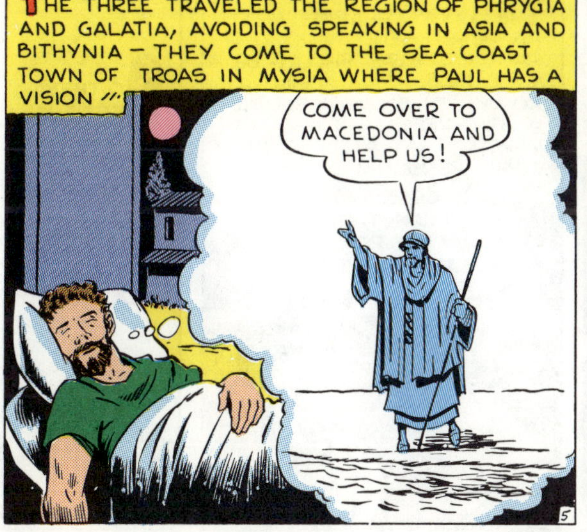

Acts 15:30-41, Acts 16:1-10

So SAILING FROM TROAS IN A STRAIGHT COURSE TO SAMOTHRACIA, THEY ARRIVED THE NEXT DAY AT NEAPOLIS AND THEN GO TO PHILIPPI, CHIEF CITY OF MACEDONIA
WE ARE GLAD ON THIS SABBATH DAY TO HOLD A MEETING TO WORSHIP GOD AND EXPLAIN WHY WE HAVE COME!
I AM LYDIA FROM THYATIRA — A SELLER OF PURPLE CLOTH — MY HEART HAS BEEN TOUCHED — I WANT YOU TO COME TO MY HOME AND BAPTIZE ME AND MY HOUSEHOLD!

So THE THREE STAY AT LYDIA'S HOME WHILE THEY PREACH IN THE CITY — A STRANGE WOMAN KEEPS FOLLOWING AND INTERRUPTING PAUL
THESE MEN ARE SERVANTS OF GOD AND SHOW US THE WAY OF SALVATION!
SHE HAS AN EVIL SPIRIT — BY FORTUNE TELLING SHE EARNS A LOT OF MONEY FOR HER MASTERS!
I COMMAND THE EVIL SPIRIT THAT POSSESSES YOU, TO COME OUT!

THE EVIL SPIRIT COMES OUT, AND HER MASTERS ARE ANGRY BECAUSE SHE NO LONGER WOULD EARN MONEY FOR THEM — THEY TAKE PAUL AND SILAS BEFORE THE CITY MAGISTRATES
THESE MEN ARE BRINGING TROUBLE TO OUR CITY, WITH TEACHINGS UNLAWFUL TO US ROMANS!

THEY ARE THROWN INTO PRISON WITH THEIR FEET MADE FAST IN STOCKS — AT MIDNIGHT WHILE PAUL AND SILAS ARE SINGING AND PRAYING, AN EARTHQUAKE BREAKS OPEN THE DOORS AND LOOSENS THEIR FEET — THE FRIGHTENED JAILER NEARBY DRAWS HIS SWORD TO KILL HIMSELF
JAILER, DON'T HARM YOURSELF WE HAVE NOT ESCAPED!

FRIGHTENED AND CONVINCED THAT THESE ARE MEN OF GOD AND CONSCIOUS OF HIS SINS HE CRIES OUT —
BUT WHAT MUST I DO TO BE SAVED?
BELIEVE ON THE LORD JESUS CHRIST AND YOU AND YOUR HOUSEHOLD WILL BE SAVED!
COME HOME I'LL CARE FOR YOUR BLEEDING BACKS, THEN STAY ALL NIGHT AND WE WILL RETURN TO THE JAIL IN THE MORNING!

THE JUDGES HEARING WHAT HAPPENED SEND WORD THAT PAUL AND SILAS SHOULD BE MADE FREE — PAUL, BEING A ROMAN CITIZEN AS WELL AS A JEW, REFUSES TO GO AND INSISTS THAT A JUDGE MUST COME PERSONALLY AND APOLOGIZE —
WE DID NOT KNOW YOU WERE ROMANS PLEASE LEAVE OUR CITY!
So THEY LEFT THE PRISON AND RETURNED TO LYDIA'S HOUSE, WHERE AFTER A BRIEF STAY THEY JOURNEY ON

AFTER TRAVELING NORTHEAST THROUGH AMPHIPOLIS AND APOLLONIA, THE THREE COME TO THESSALONICA. FOR THREE SABBATHS THEY SPEAK IN A SYNAGOGUE '''
I HAVE SHOWN THAT JESUS IS THE CHRIST FORETOLD IN OUR SCRIPTURES!
HIS WORDS ARE CONVINCING!
I AM A GREEK BUT HIS TALK APPEALS TO ME TOO!

THE RELIGIOUS LEADERS, JEALOUS OF THE SUCCESS OF THE VISITORS, PLOT TO DRIVE THEM OUT OF THEIR CITY '''
WE MUST DO SOMETHING TO PREVENT THE SPREAD OF THIS HERESY!
YOU CAN COUNT ON US!

A CROWD GATHERS AT THE HOUSE OF JASON WHERE PAUL AND SILAS ARE BEING ENTERTAINED
BRING OUT THE TRAITORS!
WE ARE COMING IN TO GET THEM!

BUT JASON HELPS THEM ESCAPE BEFORE THE CROWD COMES — JASON IS ROUGHLY HANDLED AND IS BROUGHT BEFORE THE RULERS OF THE CITY '''
I'M A RESPECTED CITIZEN, LOYAL TO OUR ROMAN LAWS — I SIMPLY GAVE LODGING TO THESE VISITORS, WHO CAME TO HELP US WITH A MESSAGE!
YES, BUT THEY SAY THAT ONE JESUS SHOULD BE OUR KING!
THIS IS DISLOYAL TO CAESAR!

JASON GIVES SECURITY GUARANTEEING GOOD BEHAVIOR WHILE PAUL AND SILAS ESCAPE '''
DOWN THAT ROAD YOU WILL REACH BEREA!

BUT THEY ARE FOLLOWED INTO BEREA BY MEN FROM THESSALONICA DETERMINED TO PERSECUTE THEM '''
I PLAN TO GO TO ATHENS BUT YOU, SILAS AND TIMOTHY, STAY HERE — BE FAITHFUL IN YOUR PREACHING — I'LL SEND FOR YOU!
GOD PROTECT YOU — MAY YOU HELP OTHERS AS YOU HAVE US!
WE WILL NEVER FORGET YOU!

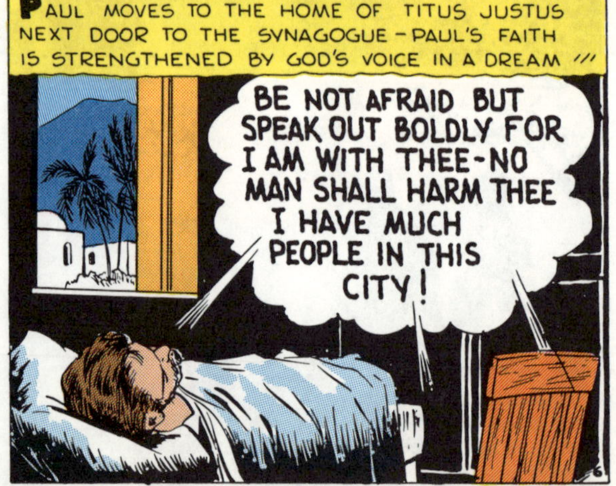

Acts 17:16-34, Acts 18:1-11

ENEMIES OF PAUL INCREASE — HE IS ARRESTED AND BROUGHT BEFORE GALLIO, THE ROMAN PRO-CONSUL OF THE PROVINCE OF ARCHAIA...
I AM HERE SIR WITH SOSTHENES, THE NEW RULER OF THE SYNAGOGUE — WE ACCUSE THIS TROUBLE MAKER OF PERSUADING OUR PEOPLE TO WORSHIP CONTRARY TO OUR LAWS!
MAY I SAY...
I AM NOT HERE TO JUDGE YOUR RELIGIOUS LAWS! YOU ARE WASTING MY TIME — GET OUT!

SYMPATHIZERS OF PAUL THROW OUT HIS ACCUSERS
YOUR WICKED PLANS DID NOT WORK!
THIS IS TO HELP YOU, FASTER!
DON'T HURT HIM!

PAUL DECIDES TO LEAVE CORINTH AND SAIL FOR HOME — HE TAKES PRISCILLA AND AQUILA ALONG
WE WILL STOP AT EPHESUS AND ENCOURAGE THE FAITH OF THE DISCIPLES!
MY SHAVEN HEAD SHOWS THAT I MADE A VOW TO SERVE GOD ANYWHERE!
WE GO WITH YOU GLADLY!

THE CHRISTIANS IN EPHESUS ARE OVERJOYED TO SEE PAUL AGAIN — THEY URGE HIM TO REMAIN, BUT HE INSISTS ON GOING TO JERUSALEM TO ATTEND THE FEAST OF THE PASSOVER...
AS I LEAVE, I REMIND YOU AGAIN OF THE UNSPEAKABLE RICHES OF CHRIST. REMAIN FAITHFUL TO HIM!

PAUL LEAVES AQUILA AND PRISCILLA BEHIND AND HE SETS SAIL...
WE'LL CARRY ON AS BEST WE CAN!
BE SURE TO COME BACK AS SOON AS POSSIBLE!
GOD WILLING I'LL RETURN TO YOU AGAIN!

SO PAUL, AFTER STOPPING AT CAESAREA AND JERUSALEM ARRIVES AT ANTIOCH, THEREBY COMPLETING HIS SECOND MISSIONARY JOURNEY
MY DEAR BRETHREN OF ANTIOCH, YOUR PRAYERS FOR ME ON MY TRIP HAVE BEEN ANSWERED — MANY CAME TO BELIEVE ON JESUS

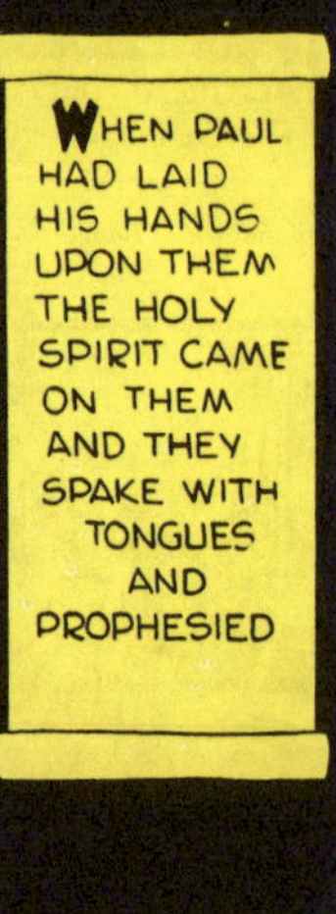

Acts 18:23-28 Acts 19:1-9

FOR MORE THAN TWO YEARS PAUL PREACHED IN EPHESUS AND THE SURROUNDING TOWNS — MANY BECOME CHRISTIANS, SOME ARE HEALED
THAT IS PAUL — HE NOT ONLY PREACHES BUT HEALS ALSO!
YES AND IT IS REPORTED THAT ANYTHING HE TOUCHES, LIKE A HANDKERCHIEF, HAS HEALING POWER!

TWO SONS OF A HIGH PRIEST WHO SEE PAUL DRIVE EVIL SPIRITS OUT OF PEOPLE, THINK THEY CAN DO IT ALSO '''
I ADJURE THE EVIL SPIRIT THAT IS IN YOU TO COME OUT IN THE NAME OF JESUS WHOM PAUL PREACHES
JESUS I KNOW, AND PAUL I KNOW, BUT WHO ARE YOU?
THAT'S THE EVIL SPIRIT SPEAKING!

MUCH TO THEIR SURPRISE THE EVIL-POSSESSED MAN LEAPS ON THEM, TEARING THEIR CLOTHES AND DRIVING THEM OUT '''
YOU CAN'T USE GOD'S SPIRIT TO EXPERIMENT ON ME!

PAUL SPEAKS SO EFFECTIVELY AGAINST THE EVILS OF MAGIC AND QUEER PRACTICES, THAT THE OWNERS OF SUCH BOOKS BRING AND BURN THEM BEFORE PAUL '''
THIS IS THE BEST EVIDENCE OF YOUR TRUE BELIEF IN GOD AND THE FOOLISHNESS OF SOOTHSAYING!
FROM NOW ON I BELIEVE IN GOD AND NOT IN SUPERSTITIONS!
THESE BOOKS WERE WORTH A LOT, ABOUT 50,000 PIECES OF SILVER!

THESE TEACHINGS INTERFERE WITH THE PROFIT-ABLE BUSINESS OF A SILVERSMITH DEMETRIUS, WHO MAKES SMALL SHRINES OF THE GODDESS DIANA — HE CALLS TOGETHER MEN IN HIS TRADE '''
SIRS, THIS MAN PAUL IS KILLING OUR BUSINESS — HE SAYS THERE ARE NO GODS WHICH ARE MADE BY HAND!
YES, AND HE BRINGS DISRESPECT UPON THE GREAT GODDESS DIANA — HE WOULD DESTROY HER MAGNIFICENCE WHICH ALL ASIA AND THE WORLD WORSHIP!

THE WHOLE CITY IS AN UPROAR — PEOPLE RUSH OUT INTO THE STREET — A LARGE ASSEMBLY GATHERS IN THE THEATER — THE TOWN CLERK QUIETS THEM '''
GREAT IS DIANA OF THE EPHESIANS!
IF DEMETRIUS AND THE CRAFTSMEN HAVE A MATTER AGAINST ANY MAN LET HIM GO ABOUT IT LAWFULLY IN OUR ASSEMBLY — THIS RIOTING MAY GET YOU INTO TROUBLE — ALL OF YOU GO HOME!
THAT SOUNDS REASONABLE
DIANA WHO CAME DOWN FROM JUPITER IS STRONG ENOUGH TO DEFEND HERSELF!

AFTER THIS UPROAR PAUL CALLS TOGETHER HIS FOLLOWERS
I AM GOING TO LEAVE EPHESUS — I WILL VISIT MACEDONIA AND GREECE — SOME OF YOU MAY WISH TO GO WITH ME AND VISIT PHILIPPI AND TROAS!
I WOULD LIKE TO GO, TOO!
I TOO!

IN TROAS PAUL STAYS A WEEK AND THEN GIVES A FAREWELL TALK ""
TOMORROW I LEAVE YOU, I HAVE MUCH TO SAY!
HE'S TALKING LONG — IT'S MIDNIGHT NOW!
THERE'S EUTYCHUS ASLEEP UP THERE ON THE WINDOW — OH, HE'S FALLING!

EUTYCHUS, LOSING HIS BALANCE, FALLS AND IS PICKED UP AS DEAD ""
THERE IS STILL LIFE IN HIM!
LOOK HE IS OPENING HIS EYES!
HE'LL LIVE ALRIGHT

THE NEXT MORNING PAUL BIDS HIS FRIENDS FAREWELL TO RETURN TO JERUSALEM TO ATTEND THE CELEBRATION OF THE DAY OF PENTECOST — EN ROUTE HE STOPS AT ASSOS, MITYLENE, CHIOS, SAMOS, TROGYLLIUM AND MILETUS WHERE HE SENDS FOR THE ELDERS OF EPHESUS ""
NOW BRETHREN, WITH SADNESS AFTER THREE YEARS I LEAVE KNOWING I SHALL NOT SEE YOU AGAIN — I ENTRUST THE BELIEVERS TO YOUR CARE — I COMMEND YOU TO GOD — SUPPORT THE WEAK — REMEMBER OUR LORD JESUS' WORDS — "IT IS MORE BLESSED TO GIVE THAN TO RECEIVE"!
HE WORKED CONSTANTLY FOR OTHERS — A GOOD EXAMPLE OF A CHRISTIAN!
HE GAVE HIS BEST, NEVER COUNTING EVEN HIS OWN LIFE DEAR TO HIMSELF!

PAUL PRAYS WITH THEM
OH GOD, GRACIOUSLY WATCH OVER THESE THY CHILDREN — MAY THY HOLY SPIRIT KEEP THEM WHEN TEMPTED TO DEPART FROM THE FAITH — AND WHEN MEN SPEAK PERVERSE THINGS TO DRAW THEM AWAY!
"AND THEY ALL WEPT SORE, AND FELL ON PAUL'S NECK AND KISSED HIM, SORROWING MOST OF ALL FOR THE WORDS WHICH HE SPAKE, THAT THEY SHOULD SEE HIS FACE NO MORE "

Acts 20:1-38

PAUL RETURNS FROM EPHESUS TO JERUSALEM. HE GOES FIRST BY WATER TO CAESAREA ///
"WE CAME WITH A STRAIGHT COURSE TO COOS, THE FOLLOWING DAY TO RHODES, THEN TO PATARA—WE CHANGED TO A SHIP SAILING FOR PHENICIA AND PASSED CYPRUS ON OUR LEFT BEFORE WE REACHED TYRE IN SYRIA. THERE WE STAYED SEVEN DAYS AND THEN REACHED PTOLEMAIS—AFTER ONE DAY WE WENT ON TO CAESAREA."

WHILE AT CAESAREA, A PROPHET NAMED AGABUS FROM JUDEA REMOVES PAUL'S BELT AND BINDS HIS OWN HANDS AND FEET ///
SO SHALL THE JEWS AT JERUSALEM BIND YOU AND DELIVER YOU TO THE GENTILES!
DON'T TAKE ANY CHANCES! —STAY HERE WITH US!
I'M GOING TO JERUSALEM, FOR I AM READY NOT TO BE BOUND ONLY, BUT ALSO TO DIE FOR THE LORD JESUS!

IN JERUSALEM, THE DISCIPLES RECEIVE HIM GLADLY, SOME WARN HIM ///
YOUR GREETINGS CHEER ME—GOD HAS BLESSED MY MINISTRY AMONG THE GENTILES!
BUT THE JEWS HERE ACCUSE YOU OF FAVORING THE GENTILES!
YES AND TELLING JEWS TO FORSAKE THE TEACHINGS OF MOSES!

THE DISCIPLES SUGGEST A PLAN TO SHOW PAUL'S LOYALTY TO THE JEWISH TRADITIONS ///
GO INTO THE TEMPLE TOMORROW WITH FOUR DEVOUT JEWS WHO WILL OBSERVE OUR TRADITIONS EVEN TO SHAVING THEIR HEADS AS A VOW TO GOD!
STAY WITH THEM THE SEVEN DAYS OF PURIFICATION— THEN NO ONE CAN SAY YOU ARE A DISLOYAL JEW!

BUT CERTAIN JEWS FROM ASIA ARE DETERMINED TO MAKE TROUBLE FOR PAUL—THEY GRAB HIM AND CRY OUT ///
MEN OF ISRAEL, HELP!—THIS MAN IS VIOLATING OUR LAWS!
HE MINGLES WITH GREEKS AND EVEN BRINGS THEM HERE INTO OUR TEMPLE!

IN ANGER THEY THREW PAUL OUT AND ATTACK HIM—— SOLDIERS COME TO HIS RESCUE ///
IF THERE'S TO BE ANY PUNISHMENT WE'LL DO IT!
HE'S A TROUBLE MAKER!

AS PAUL IS BOUND AND CARRIED INTO THE CASTLE HE SPEAKS TO THE CAPTAIN IN GREEK
MAY I SPEAK TO THE PEOPLE AND EXPLAIN? I'M A CITIZEN OF TARSUS!
YOU SPEAK GREEK!—I THOUGHT YOU WERE THAT EGYPTIAN WHO STARTED AN INSURRECTION WITH 4000 FOLLOWERS WHO WERE MURDERERS!

Acts 21:39-40; Acts 22:1-30; Acts 23:1-3

PAUL APOLOGIZES TO THE HIGH PRIEST AND THEN NOTICES THERE ARE BOTH PHARISEES AND SADDUCEES IN THE COUNCIL ~
I AM A PHARISEE AND BECAUSE I BELIEVE IN A RESURRECTION OF THE DEAD I AM BEING TRIED!
I, A PHARISEE, THINK HE HAS A RIGHT TO THAT BELIEF!
I DIFFER—IT'S A CRAZY IDEA AS IS ALSO HIS BELIEF IN VISIONS!

THIS STARTED A CONTROVERSY SINCE THE SADDUCEES SAY THERE IS NO RESURRECTION NOR ANGELS WHILE THE PHARISEES BELIEVE IN BOTH ~
WE FIND NO EVIL IN THIS MAN!
IF A SPIRIT OR AN ANGEL SPOKE TO HIM, LET US NOT OPPOSE GOD!

AS THE ARGUMENTS BECOME MORE HEATED AND THERE IS DANGER OF PHYSICAL VIOLENCE TO PAUL, THE CAPTAIN ORDERS HIS SOLDIERS TO TAKE HIM FROM THE COUNCIL ~

THE LORD SPOKE TO PAUL THAT NIGHT IN A DREAM
BE OF GOOD CHEER, PAUL--AS THOU HAST TESTIFIED OF ME IN JERUSALEM, SO MUST THOU BEAR WITNESS ALSO AT ROME

A DISGRUNTLED GROUP BANDS TOGETHER AND PLOTS AGAINST PAUL – HIS SISTER'S SON OVERHEARS THE PLOT ~
FORTY OF US HAVE TAKEN AN OATH TO EAT NOTHING UNTIL WE HAVE GOTTEN PAUL!
I'LL TELL PAUL IMMEDIATELY!

PAUL HEARS THE STORIES AND ARRANGES FOR HIS NEPHEW TO REPORT IT TO THE CHIEF CAPTAIN ~
TAKE THIS YOUNG MAN TO THE CHIEF CAPTAIN– HE HAS SOMETHING OF IMPORTANCE TO SAY!

Acts 23:19-35, Acts 24:1-14

PAUL INSISTS THAT IT IS BECAUSE OF HIS BELIEF IN THE RESURRECTION THAT HE IS BEING PERSECUTED '''
I WAS IN THE TEMPLE PRESENTING MY GIFTS, WHEN CERTAIN MEN FROM ASIA GRABBED ME AND BROUGHT FALSE CHARGES AGAINST ME BEFORE THEIR COUNCIL — THERE I SAID I BELIEVED IN THE RESURRECTION!
TELL ME AND MY WIFE DRUSILLA ABOUT YOUR BELIEFS

AND AS HE REASONED OF RIGHTEOUSNESS TEMPERANCE, AND JUDGMENT TO COME, FELIX TREMBLED AND ANSWERED: "GO YOUR WAY FOR THIS TIME, WHEN I HAVE A CONVENIENT SEASON I WILL CALL FOR YOU"

FELIX KEEPS PAUL CONFINED FOR TWO YEARS, HOPING THAT HE WILL PAY TO BE RELEASED ~
I CANNOT COMPLAIN — FELIX GIVES ME LIBERTIES, HE SAYS HE POSTPONES MY TRIAL UNTIL LYSIAS, THE CHIEF CAPTAIN, COMES TO GIVE FURTHER FACTS!
IF YOU PAID HIM HE WOULD LET YOU OUT!

PORCIUS FESTUS SUCCEEDS FELIX — WHILE IN JERUSALEM PAUL'S ACCUSERS APPROACH HIM '''
MOST NOBLE FESTUS, WE DESIRE A SMALL FAVOR — SEND PAUL HERE TO BE TRIED!
NO! — I'M RETURNING TO CAESAREA SHORTLY — COME ALONG AND I'LL TRY HIM THERE!
ANOTHER PLAN TO WAYLAY PAUL IS FOILED!

FESTUS, A DAY AFTER HE ARRIVES, HOLDS COURT TO TRY PAUL BEFORE HIS ACCUSERS ~
NONE OF THE ACCUSATIONS CAN BE PROVED, I HAVE VIOLATED NO LAWS OF THE JEWS, THE TEMPLE, NOR OF CAESAR!
ARE YOU WILLING THEN TO BE TRIED IN JERUSALEM?

PAUL STANDS FOR HIS RIGHTS AS A ROMAN CITIZEN AND DEMANDS THAT HE BE TRIED IN ROME '''
I THOUGHT I WAS HERE AT ONE OF CAESAR'S COURTS — I HAVE DONE NO WRONG TO MY FELLOW JEWS — I DO NOT REFUSE TO DIE IF I HAVE DONE ANYTHING WORTHY OF DEATH — I THEREFORE APPEAL TO CAESAR!
SINCE YOU APPEAL TO CAESAR, TO ROME YOU WILL GO!

Acts 25:13-27 Acts 26:1-21

I PREACH WHAT MOSES SAID WOULD COME TO PASS, THAT CHRIST SHOULD SUFFER AND THAT HE SHOULD RISE FROM THE DEAD AND BE A LIGHT UNTO ALL PEOPLE!
LOOK, GOVERNOR FESTUS IS GETTING EXCITED!
PAUL, YOU ARE BESIDE YOURSELF! MUCH LEARNING HAS MADE YOU MAD!

MOST NOBLE FESTUS, I AM NOT MAD BUT SPEAK WORDS OF TRUTH AND SOBERNESS — THE KING KNOWS, FOR THEY WERE DONE OPENLY!

KING AGRIPPA, DO YOU BELIEVE WHAT THE PROPHETS WROTE? — I KNOW YOU DO!
PAUL, YOU ALMOST PERSUADE ME TO BECOME A CHRISTIAN!

I WOULD TO GOD THAT NOT ONLY YOU, BUT ALL WHO HEAR, WERE NOT ALMOST, BUT ENTIRELY DECIDED LIKE ME, EXCEPT NOT TO BE UNDER ARREST!

THE KING, HIS WIFE AND THE GOVERNOR CONFER
NO WONDER THIS MAN WINS SO MANY BELIEVERS!
HE HAS NOT COMMITTED ANY CRIME!

I AM SORRY! I COULD RELEASE HIM IF HE HAD NOT APPEALED TO CAESAR!

THE DAY CAME WHEN PAUL WITH OTHER PRISONERS SET SAIL FOR ITALY ...
WE SAIL FROM CAESAREA STOPPING FIRST AT SIDON THEN ALONG THE COAST OF ASIA!
PAUL WAS ENTRUSTED TO A ROMAN CENTURION, JULIUS, WHO SHOWS KINDNESS

AT SIDON PAUL IS ALLOWED TO HAVE FRIENDS VISIT HIM ...
I GO TO ROME, THE HEART OF THE EMPIRE WHERE I WILL PROCLAIM THE GOSPEL!
SEND US WORD BY SOMEONE RETURNING!

"...FROM SIDON WE SAILED UNDER THE LEE OF CYPRUS BECAUSE OF CONTRARY WINDS, THEN ON THE SEA OFF CILICIA AND PAMPHYLIA TO MYRA, A CITY OF LYCIA. THERE WE CHANGED TO A SHIP SAILING FOR ITALY, NEXT SAILING SLOWLY OVER AGAINST CNIDUS AND THEN UNDER CRETE OVER AGAINST SALMONE. COASTING ALONG WE CAME TO A PLACE FAIR HAVENS NEAR THE CITY OF LASEA"
AT LYSEA BECAUSE OF CONTINUING STORMY WEATHER, PAUL URGES THE SHIP'S MASTER TO DELAY SAILING ...
WE SHOULD STAY HERE OR WE MAY LOSE OUR CARGO AND EVEN OUR LIVES!
THIS IS NOT A GOOD HARBOR AND WE HAVE OUR CARGO TO DELIVER AT PHENICE IN CRETE!

SO WHEN A SOUTH WIND BLOWS THEY SAIL ALONG THE COAST OF CRETE "
THIS IS BEAUTIFUL SAILING WEATHER!

THE MILD SOFT WIND SOON CHANGES TO A TEMPESTUOUS STORM – THE CAPTAIN THUNDERS OUT ORDERS "
SIR, THERE AHEAD IS THE ISLAND OF CLAUDA I BELIEVE!

AS SOON AS THE WIND ABATES WE MUST PUT CHAINS AND ROPES AROUND THE HULL AND REEF SAIL LEST WE RUN ON TO QUICK SAND!

Acts 27:1-18

THE SEVERE STORM CONTINUES — ON THE THIRD DAY THE CAPTAIN CALLS THE CREW AND PASSENGERS TOGETHER '''
YESTERDAY, TO LIGHTEN THE SHIP WE THREW THE CARGO OVERBOARD—— TODAY WE MUST THROW OVER THE BLOCKS, ROPES AND TACKLE!
WE HAVE NOT SEEN THE SUN NOR THE STARS FOR DAYS!

AS ALL HOPE FOR THE SHIP IS LOST, PAUL SPEAKS TO THE CROWD
IF I HAD BEEN OBEYED AT CRETE WE WOULD NOT SUFFER ALL THIS LOSS — BUT BE OF GOOD CHEER FOR NONE OF YOU WILL BE DROWNED!

AND PAUL GAVE HIS REASON FOR CONFIDENCE
THERE STOOD BY ME THIS NIGHT AN ANGEL OF GOD SAYING 'FEAR NOT, PAUL, YOU MUST BE BROUGHT BEFORE CAESAR; GOD HATH GIVEN THEE ALL WHO SAIL WITH THEE!'

ON THE 14TH NIGHT AT MIDNIGHT A SAILOR SEES LAND AHEAD '''
CAPTAIN, WE ARE APPROACHING LAND!
WHAT ARE THE SOUNDINGS?
ONLY FIFTEEN FATHOMS RIGHT NOW, IT WAS TWENTY PREVIOUSLY!

THROW OUT FOUR ANCHORS ASTERN LEST WE RUN ON THE ROCKS!
LET'S ROW AWAY IN ONE OF THE SMALL BOATS, SAYING WE INTEND TO CAST OFF ANOTHER ANCHOR FROM THE PROW!

PAUL OVERHEARS THEIR PLANS TO ESCAPE AND SPEAKS TO THE CENTURION AND THE SOLDIERS '''
UNLESS THOSE MEN STAY ABOARD, THE REST OF US WILL ALL BE LOST!
I'LL FIX THAT BY CUTTING THIS ROPE TO THE BOAT!

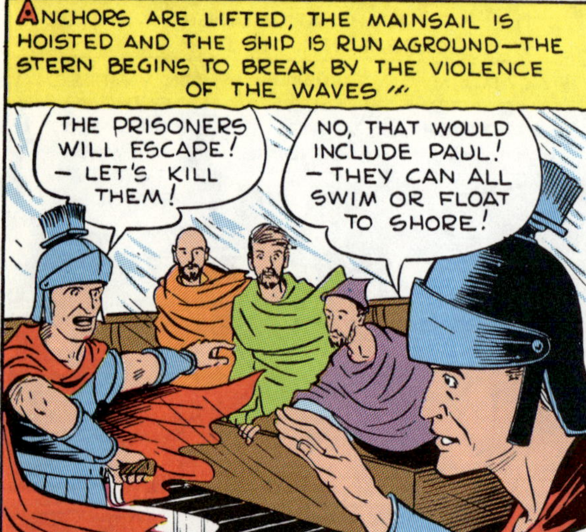

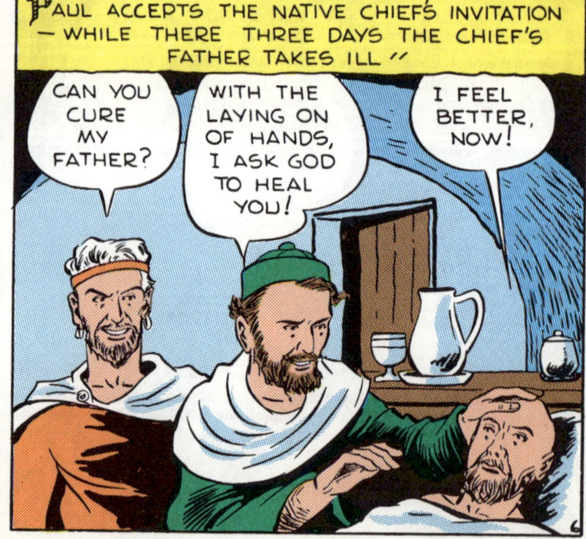

Acts 27:33-44; Acts 28:1-8

WITH THE HEALING OF THE CHIEF'S FATHER, MANY OTHERS ARE BROUGHT TO PAUL FOR HEALING
HE'S HEALED ME!
AND ME, TOO!

AFTER THREE MONTHS A SHIP SAILING FOR ROME ARRIVES — GRATEFUL NATIVES SHOWER GIFTS UPON PAUL AS HE LEAVES
THESE PRESENTS ARE FOR YOU!
GOD BLESS YOU AND HELP YOU TO REMEMBER ALL I'VE TAUGHT YOU ABOUT JESUS!

ON THE TRIP TO ROME THE SHIP STOPPED AT SYRACUSE, RHEGIUM AND PUTEOLI
THEN WITH FRIENDS THEY TRAVELED OVERLAND TO ROME

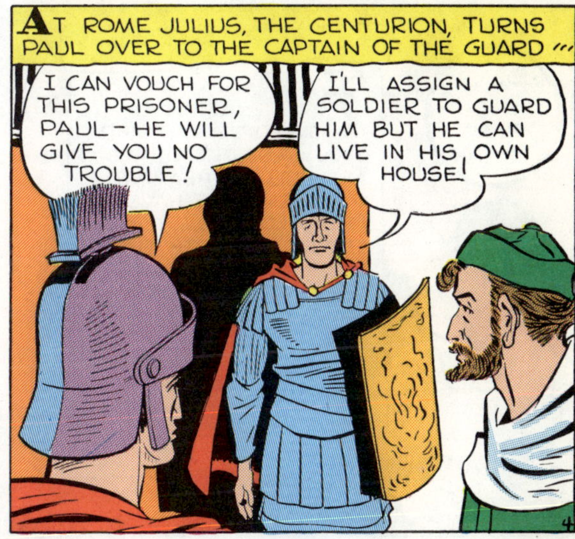
AT ROME JULIUS, THE CENTURION, TURNS PAUL OVER TO THE CAPTAIN OF THE GUARD
I CAN VOUCH FOR THIS PRISONER, PAUL — HE WILL GIVE YOU NO TROUBLE!
I'LL ASSIGN A SOLDIER TO GUARD HIM BUT HE CAN LIVE IN HIS OWN HOUSE!

PAUL CALLS THE CHIEF JEWS TOGETHER AFTER THREE DAYS, TO EXPLAIN WHY HE IS THERE
MEN AND BRETHREN, THOUGH I HAVE COMMITTED NO CRIME AGAINST JEWS OR ROMANS, I AM BROUGHT HERE A PRISONER, BECAUSE I APPEALED TO CAESAR!

WE HAVE HAD NO LETTERS FROM JUDEA ABOUT THIS, NOR ANY ADVANCE NOTICE OF YOUR COMING!
YOU APPOINT A DAY AND WE'LL MEET AGAIN!

SO PAUL INVITES IMPORTANT JEWS TO HIS HOUSE—THEY STAY THERE ALL DAY '''
I WILL EXPLAIN HOW THE KINGDOM OF GOD THAT I PREACH WAS TAUGHT BY MOSES, AND THE PROPHETS!

SOME OF THESE JEWS IN ROME BELIEVE, BUT OTHERS DO NOT '''
IN CONCLUSION I SAY THAT IN JESUS ALL THE LAWS OF MOSES AND THE PROPHETS ARE FULFILLED!
IF IT IS TRUE, WHY THEN DO SO MANY JEWS REJECT THESE TEACHINGS?

PAUL READS FROM ISAIAH
"FOR THE HEART OF THIS PEOPLE IS WAXED GROSS, AND THEIR EARS ARE DULL OF HEARING, AND THEIR EYES HAVE THEY CLOSED; LEST THEY SHOULD SEE WITH THEIR EYES, AND HEAR WITH THEIR EARS, AND UNDERSTAND WITH THEIR HEART, AND SHOULD BE CONVERTED, AND I SHOULD HEAL THEM."

AS THEY LEAVE PAUL REMINDS THEM THAT THE GENTILES EAGERLY RECEIVE HIS MESSAGE'''
YOU HAVE QUESTIONED ALL THAT I HAVE EXPLAINED, BUT THE GENTILES WILL HEAR AND BELIEVE!
WE WILL DISCUSS THIS AMONG OURSELVES!

SO LUKE HERE CONCLUDES HIS ACCOUNT RECORDED IN THE ACTS OF THE APOSTLES '''
"AND PAUL DWELT TWO WHOLE YEARS IN HIS OWN HIRED HOUSE AND RECEIVED ALL THAT CAME IN UNTO HIM PREACHING THE KINGDOM OF GOD"

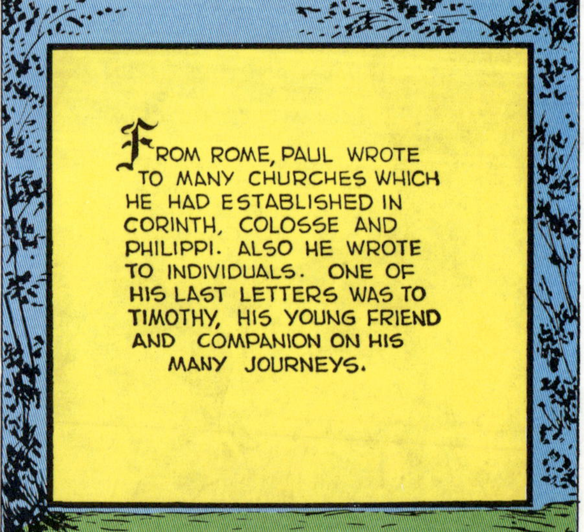
FROM ROME, PAUL WROTE TO MANY CHURCHES WHICH HE HAD ESTABLISHED IN CORINTH, COLOSSE AND PHILIPPI. ALSO HE WROTE TO INDIVIDUALS. ONE OF HIS LAST LETTERS WAS TO TIMOTHY, HIS YOUNG FRIEND AND COMPANION ON HIS MANY JOURNEYS.

TIMOTHY SHOWS HIS LETTER TO HIS MOTHER, EUNICE
A GREAT SURPRISE — A SECOND LETTER FROM PAUL IN ROME!
OH, LET'S READ IT AT ONCE!

TO TIMOTHY, MY OWN SON IN THE FAITH, STAY IN EPHESUS AND TELL THE PEOPLE THERE ABOUT THE TEACHINGS OF JESUS YOU LEARNED FROM ME ON OUR TRAVELS.

TIMOTHY SPEAKS FIRST TO THE OFFICERS OF THE CHURCH IN EPHESUS ~~~
OUR BELOVED PAUL KEEPS US CONSTANTLY IN MIND — HE WARNS US NOT TO LISTEN TO ANY FALSE TEACHINGS — SEE WHAT HE SAYS HERE!
ELDERS MUST BE BLAMELESS, SOBER, NOT QUARRELSOME, NOT GREEDY!

WHAT DOES HE SAY ABOUT US DEACONS?
BE CAREFUL NOT TO SPEAK EVIL — RULE YOUR OWN FAMILY WELL — TAKE GOOD CARE OF MONEY COLLECTED FOR THE WIDOWS AND THE POOR!

TIMOTHY CALLS THE YOUNG PEOPLE OF THE CHURCH TOGETHER ~~~
I HAD EXCITING TIMES TRAVELLING WITH PAUL — SOME PEOPLE STONED US AND CHASED US OUT OF THEIR CITIES!
WHY DID YOU GO ON THESE DANGEROUS TRIPS?

TIMOTHY EXPLAINS HOW AS A YOUNG MAN IN DERBE HE MET PAUL, WHOSE COURAGE AND ADVENTUROUS TRIPS APPEALED TO HIM ~~
PAUL TOLD US THE SECRET OF A HAPPY LIFE — I DECIDED THEN TO BE A CHRISTIAN, AS DID MY GRANDMOTHER LOIS AND MY MOTHER!

II Timothy 4:2-5, Matthew 19:13-15, Ephesians 6:1-4, II Timothy 1:1-5

AMONG PAUL'S LAST WORDS TO TIMOTHY WERE THESE: "I HAVE FOUGHT A GOOD FIGHT, I HAVE FINISHED MY COURSE; I HAVE KEPT THE FAITH. HENCEFORTH THERE IS LAID UP FOR ME A CROWN OF RIGHTEOUSNESS."

The End

EDITORIAL ADVISORY COUNCIL
for
Picture Stories from the Bible:
The New Testament in full-color comic-strip form

Dr. William Ward Ayer
Pastor, Calvary Baptist Church, New York City

Raimundo deOvies
Dean —Cathedral of St. Philip, Atlanta, Georgia

Dorothy Canfield Fisher
Editor, Author and Translator

Prof. Samuel L. Hamilton
Chairman, Department of Religious Education, New York University, and Chairman, Committee on Research, International Council of Religious Education

Frank S. Mead
Editor, The Christian Herald

Dr. J. Quinter Miller
Associate General Secretary, Federal Council of the Churches of Christ in America, in Charge of Field Work

Dr. Norman Vincent Peale
Minister, Marble Collegiate Church, New York City, and Author of ''The Art of Living'' and other books

Dr. Francis C. Stifler
Secretary for Public Relations, American Bible Society

Edward L. Wertheim
Secretary to Advisory Council
Former President, Bible School Superintendents' Union of New York

The positions given for the members of the Advisory Council are those held in 1946, when this book was originally published. Members served in a voluntary capacity as individuals, and their presence did not necessarily mean the endorsement of the organizations they represented.

OLD TESTAMENT EDITION

"Picture Stories from the Bible: the *Old Testament* in full-color comic-strip form" is also available. For information about this 224-page book and the name of the bookseller nearest you, write to Scarf Press, 58 East 83rd Street, New York, New York 10028.